# Under the Black Mountains:
## The History of Gwernyfed since 1600

*In memory of Vicar and Mrs Lewis*
*of Glasbury*

# Under the Black Mountains:
## The History of Gwernyfed since 1600

*Edited by*
Colin A. Lewis

**Logaston Press**

LOGASTON PRESS
Little Logaston Woonton Almeley
Herefordshire HR3 6QH
logastonpress.co.uk

First published by Logaston Press 2017
Copyright text as printed here © Colin Lewis
Copyright illustrations © as per credits and acknowledgements

ISBN 978 1 910839 15 7

Typeset by Logaston Press
and printed and bound in Poland by
www.lfbookservices.co.uk

*Front cover:*
*Top: Old Gwernyfed in the second decade of the 21st century. (Photo by Colin Lewis)*
*Bottom: Gwernyfed Park by A.R. Quinton.*
*(Courtesy of the owner of the painting: Mrs Windham)*

# CONTENTS

# ACKNOWLEDGEMENTS

The sources of Figures are acknowledged in individual Figure captions. The Welsh Historic Gardens Trust and the daughter of Dr Nesta Lloyd are thanked for allowing the inclusion of Dr Lloyd's translation of the praise poem performed at festivities for the marriage of Eleanor Whitney to Sir Henry (Harry) Williams in 1605. Also thanked are Mrs Mary Mellor for providing a copy of Mrs Hore-Ruthven's typescript, the editor of *Brycheiniog* for permission to reproduce material from that journal; Mrs June Thomas for a copy of the jingle by Z.A.H. Jones entitled *Velindre Jubilee*; Velindre Hall Committee for a copy of the same author's subsequent jingle, the great-grandson of Elyned Hore-Ruthven for not objecting to publication of her story (his wish that no painting belonging to the family be included in the book has been adhered to); Dr M.A.V. Gill, former archivist of St Peter's Church, Glasbury, for her unfailing help and enthusiasm and for copies of material formerly published, or intended to be published, in *The Messenger* (the magazine of the Wye Valley Parishes); Mrs Sheila Leitch for generous help and for allowing me to consult copies of Glasbury parish registers and the sales catalogue for the auction of Gwernyfed Estate properties in 1922; Mr and Mrs Glyn Smart for information on Mrs Kinsey; Mr Dereck Price for allowing me to scan material on Glasbury bridge; Mrs Anne Goold for lending me a copy of *Gerddi*, 2005-6; Mr John Goodger, Mr Glen Smith and the management of Velindre Village Hall for allowing me to include material exhibited in Velindre Village Hall in 2016, the Reverend David Thomas (vicar of Glasbury) for allowing me to consult parish archives, the staff of The National Library of Wales, The Royal Commission on the Ancient and Historical Monuments of Wales, The National Portrait Gallery, London, the Brecknock Museum and Art Gallery and Mr William Bowker of the Glasbury History Group for aid with illustrations; my wife, Marijke Lewis, for assistance with information technology and other matters (and apologies for being so clumsy a learner). No descendants of T.P. Perks, J.W. Hobbs, and M.J. Kinsey have been found, in spite of enquiries in the Velindre/Three Cocks area, and apologies are made if any copyrights have been infringed. Members of Rhodes University, University College Dublin, the National University of Ireland Maynooth, and of The University of Wales St David's College Lampeter, are thanked for academic and other support. The publisher, Logaston Press, has been supportive and encouraging throughout the production of this book and is greatly thanked.

## Notes

The letter in Welsh that is pronounced like a v in English is now spelled, in Welsh, as f. During much of the time-period discussed in this book it was spelled by the letter v, even on official documents. For the sake of consistency the letter v will be used in this book.

In 1751 with the passing of the Calendar Act, Britain switched from the Julian Calendar to the Gregorian Calendar, meaning 11 days were omitted from September 1752, when the day after 2 September was 14 September.[1] Under the Act the start of the year was also changed, from 25 March (Lady Day) to 1 January. Thus, what would have been 1 January 1752, became 1 January 1753. The year of Sir David Williams' death is given in this book as 1613, but is shown on a side panel on his tomb in Brecon Cathedral as 1614. The panel may have been added to the tomb subsequent to the passing of the 1751 Act.

# PREFACE

The idea behind this book is to bring together the various memories of times at Gwernyfed, in Velindre, Glasbury and Three Cocks, which had been written down in the early to mid-1900s. This idea is not new. Before her death in 1965 Mrs Hore-Ruthven, a daughter of the Wood family and their ancestors who had owned the Gwernyfed estate since 1600, gave my father, the Reverend E.T.D. Lewis, vicar of the benefice within which much of the estate was located, a bound typescript copy of a manuscript that she had written for her grandchildren. She told him that he was welcome to have it published. This gave a charming account of her Victorian childhood at Gwernyfed and elsewhere. When Mrs Hore-Ruthven spoke with my father she was then residing at Old Gwernyfed. This was an Elizabethan mansion that had formerly been the centre of the estate, but which had been supplanted by two younger residences built in Gwernyfed Park: The Lodge and, subsequently, Gwernyfed Park itself. Old Gwernyfed had been relegated to a farmhouse with its own lands until Mrs Hore-Ruthven had it converted into a summer retreat in the 1930s.

My father subsequently obtained copies of essays by Thomas Perks about life at Old Gwernyfed when it was a farm, and by J.W. Hobbs about life in the Three Cocks area in the early 1900s, when he had been working at the railway station. He then persuaded Mary Kinsey to write her memories of the Gwernyfed area during Mrs Hore-Ruthven's lifetime. Lewis intended that all four manuscripts should be published as a social history of the area. He also persuaded Arthur Ivor Jacob to write 'A brief history of the Pontithel Chemical Works', which is not included in this book but is lodged in Powys Archives (No. 65 from St Peter's Church, Glasbury, archives).

Unfortunately my father died before editing the collection and guiding it through the press, although he arranged for Thomas Perks' essay to be published, serialised in the 1980s, in four issues of *The Messenger, the local magazine for everyone, from the churches of the Wye Valley Parishes*. J.W. Hobbs' essay was published in *The Messenger* in two parts, in May 1997 and in January 1998. Mrs Hilda Richards, who was then the editor of *The Messenger*, believes that extracts from Mrs Hore-Ruthven's manuscript were also published as were parts of Mary Kinsey's memories, but they have not been found in the parish archives. Mary Kinsey's typescript is now lodged in Powys Archives (No. 63 from St Peter's Church, Glasbury, archives).

To the four essays now reproduced as chapters in this book I have added a further four chapters which give a history of the Gwernyfed estate and its landowning families since 1600 when Gwernyfed Mansion (now Old Gwernyfed) was bought by David Williams, a lawyer and ancestor of Mrs Hore-Ruthven. These chapters give a background to the succeeding essays.

The four essays have been reproduced with as little change to the original text as possible; this way the four quite different voices can be heard. Obvious errors in typing up the manuscripts have been corrected, and additional information has sometimes been added, indicated by the use of square brackets around the insertions. Likewise, where some editing of the text has occurred, for example to remove some extraneous asides, square brackets are used to indicate text that forms the new link in the narrative. Two of the essays have had some additional changes. Thomas Perks subsequently produced a second essay, and text from this has been blended into his original to form a more coherent whole. To the essay by J.W. Hobbs has been added some information taken from a partially unpublished typescript of his memories in the possession of Dr M.A.V. Gill in 2016.

Much of the Gwernyfed estate was sold during the 20th century and this book is, in many ways, a memorial to a way of life that no longer exists in the Wye valley of the Welsh borderlands.

Colin A Lewis, Professor Emeritus, Rhodes University, South Africa
St David's Day, 2017

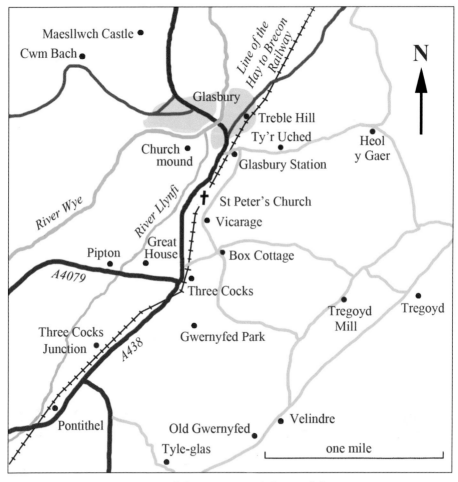

*Map of the area around Gwernyfed*

# 1   Gwernyfed prior to the death of David Williams

Gwernyfed, near Glasbury-on-Wye in the Wye valley, is best known in the second decade of the 21st century as the home of an excellent secondary school. The school opened in 1950 and was housed in the mansion of Gwernyfed Park. This mansion was built between 1877 and 1880 by Thomas IV Wood (1853-1933) as a fitting home for his wife, Rhona Cecilia Emily Tollemache (1857-1940). Over 250 years earlier, within the years 1600-1605, the mansion now known as Old Gwernyfed, located near the village of Velindre and less than a mile away from Gwernyfed Park, was built (or rebuilt) as home for Sir Henry (Harry) Williams (1579/80-1636) and his bride, Eleanor Whitney (*c*.1589-after 1663). Sir Henry's father, David Williams (1536-1613), who, like his son was knighted in 1603,[1] had

*Fig. 1.1. Old Gwernyfed c.1960, when the author of* A Victorian Childhood
*resided in the house during summer months.*
*(Reproduced by permission of the editor of* Brycheiniog*)*

1

purchased Gwernyfed from John Gunter in 1600. The Gunter family may have occupied Gwernyfed since the Norman conquest of the area, although that is not certain.

The ownership of Gwernyfed immediately prior to the Norman invasion is unclear. The Norman invaders, under Bernard Neufmarché and his supporters, conquered much of the local area at the battle of Brecon in 1093.[2] Bleddyn ap Maenarch, who may have been the leading local leader, was apparently killed in that battle. There is a tradition that Neufmarché gave at least that portion of Gwernyfed that is within the parish of Aberllynfi to Bleddyn's eldest son, Gwgan, as a show of clemency.[3]

Einion Sais ('Einion the Englishman'), thought to be a sixth generation descendant of Gwgan,[4] spent much time in England and had, as his shield, a red chevron with three red cocks on a silver background (Fig. 1.2). This shield, which subsequently formed part of the arms of Sir David Williams, is thought to be the origin of the name of the village that now exists a few hundred yards away from the ruined remains of Aberllynfi church – Three Cocks. This is also the name of the local postal district.

Whether Gwernyfed really was granted to Gwgan is uncertain, and Neufmarché may well have given it to Sir Peter Gunter, one of the knights who helped in the conquest of the area. The Gunter family occupied Gwernyfed in 1600, when (as already stated) John Gunter sold it to David Williams.[5] John had farmed land, on lease, in the adjoining Manor of Glasbury, but his lease there apparently ended before the end of the 16th century. In 1594-5 Queen Elizabeth I granted David Williams, who

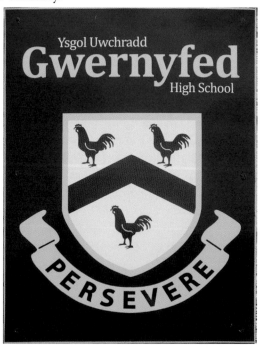

*Fig. 1.2 The shield of Einion Sais as depicted at the entrance to Gwernyfed High School in 2016. (Photo by Colin Lewis)*

was her attorney for five counties in south Wales in 1581-5, the Manor of Glasbury and other lands.[6] The loss of arable and grass land in that manor with the termination of his lease may have made it financially impossible for Gunter to continue to reside at Gwernyfed, hence its sale to David Williams.

David Williams (Fig. 1.3) was the youngest son of Gwilym ap John Vaughan of Blaen Nedd in the Ystradfellte area of Breconshire. His father has been described as 'a substantial yeoman'. In his youth David embarked on a legal career, entering the Middle Temple in 1568. He was called to the Bar in 1576, became a Serjeant-at-Law in 1593 (which enabled him to plead at Westminster, in Star Chamber and Chancery), and ended his legal career as a puisne Justice of the King's Bench, to which he was appointed in 1604. Williams amassed considerable wealth from his legal career, much of which he invested in land. From his

*Fig 1.3 The tomb of Sir David Williams and his first wife, Margery née Games of Aberbrân, in the south aisle of Brecon Cathedral. (Photo by Colin Lewis)*

second marriage, in 1597, to Dorothy the widow of John Latton of Kingston Bagpuize (then in Berkshire though, after boundary reorganization in 1974, now in Oxfordshire), he managed to accumulate estates in Berkshire and Oxfordshire in addition to the lands he held in Wales.[7]

Sir David died in 1613 and was succeeded by his son, Henry (Sir Harry). Fortunately, when Harry married in 1605, the condition of Gwernyfed and its estate was outlined in a bardic poem, in Welsh, welcoming his bride to Gwernyfed. From that poem much is known of the mansion and estate at that time, as will be described later. There is very limited evidence of what Gwernyfed looked like when bought by David Williams, but there is some timber evidence to suggest that it might have been a simple hall-type house. This type consisted of a central passage-way with a room on either side, possibly with a staircase in the passage-way leading to one or more rooms above.[8]

The history of the landowning family at Gwernyfed from Sir Harry's time onwards is known in considerable detail, as will be outlined in the following three chapters. The privileged position into which Elyned Wood, the author of *A Victorian Childhood* (see Chapter 5), was born will be shown: she was a descendant of Sir Harry. Elyned's life will be set against the tremendous periods of change through which she lived, ending in the virtual demise of the estate and semi-feudal system at Gwernyfed in the second half of the 20th century.

# 2  GWERNYFED IN THE 17TH CENTURY

An estate map of 1756 (I know of none for the 17th century) shows that Gwernyfed then included much of the Parish of Aberllynfi, east of the present village of Three Cocks, and extended into the adjoining Parish of Tregoyd and Velindre (Fig. 2.1). The mansion of Gwernyfed itself was located east of the Parish of Aberllynfi and within that of Tregoyd and Velindre. The Gwernyfed estate, however, extended much further, particularly from the escarpment of the Black Mountains to the River Wye. The exact area bought in 1600 by David Williams from John Gunter is, however, uncertain.

Sir David's eldest son, Henry (but best known as Harry), had been born c.1579/80, during the reign of Queen Elizabeth I. His mother was Margery, daughter of John Games of Aberbrân, near Brecon. The Games were a notable and respected county family in Breconshire. Harry seems to have been educated at Shrewsbury before proceeding to St John's College, Oxford. From there he entered the Middle Temple in 1594 where he remained until 1604. During this period Harry became Member of Parliament for Brecon Boroughs, a Justice of the Peace in Breconshire and, in 1603, like his father, was knighted.[1]

Whether it was Harry or his father who modernised or rebuilt the mansion at Gwernyfed is unknown, but 'From October 1604 [Harry] was consistently fined for absence from Middle Temple readings, having evidently retired to Breconshire to look after the family's Welsh interests'.[2] Perhaps he was supervising completion of the remodelled or new mansion at Gwernyfed and laying out the associated park.

In 1605 Harry married Eleanor Whitney (c.1589-1663). She was the daughter of Eustace Whitney (1545-1608) of Whitney Court in Herefordshire and Margaret the daughter of William Vaughan of Glasbury. Vaughan, the great-nephew of Blanche Parry[3] had owned Glasbury Manor, which Blanche had owned previously. (Blanche (1507/8-1590) was Chief Gentlewoman of Queen Elizabeth I's Privy Chamber, and therefore a person of great influence.) A decade after Vaughan's death in 1584 the manor was acquired by David Williams. The marriage of Harry and Eleanor was thus, in a sense, restoration to Eleanor of family lands.

As part of the wedding festivities a bard performed a praise-poem welcoming Eleanor to Gwernyfed. In Welsh society it was traditional for the *uchelwyr* (the upper groups of society) to welcome bards to their homes, and some even supported their own bards. 'Bards were honoured guests, with a place beside the master at high table in the hall. The poems,

*Fig 2.1. An estate map of Gwernyfed, dated 1756, by Robert Parry Price
and commissioned by The Honourable Sir Edward Williams, Bart.
(By permission of Llyfrgell Genedlaethol Cymru / The National Library of Wales)*

sung to a harp accompaniment, incorporated salient facts about the host and the surroundings …'.[4]

The Williams were a Welsh speaking family, although Sir David and his son are known to have also been fluent in English. The fact that a bard performed at the wedding festivities, and that he referred to the bride (as translated into English) as: 'An aristocratic, gentle Welshwoman [who will] listen to the complaints of the poor', strongly suggests that she and her family were also Welsh speaking; being bilingual was common around 1600 in Herefordshire as well as in adjacent Wales. The first full and easily readable translation of the Bible into Welsh, by Bishop Morgan, was published in 1588 especially for the people of Wales and Herefordshire.

The name of the bard is not known and only one copy of his manuscript survives. The name of the poem is 'Croeso y Wernyfed' (Welcome to Gwernyfed). Significantly, the poem includes a number of English words, and seems to have been written in the form of Welsh then used in the Brecon/Radnor border area.[5] The inclusion of English words in the poem was a forerunner of the end of the bardic tradition in the region 'when increasing Anglicisation of the ruling classes meant that noble families who had hitherto supported the bards, no longer understood and/or sufficiently valued Welsh'.[6] Nevertheless, Harry Williams was a strong supporter of the bardic tradition and long after his wedding maintained his own harpist and wrote his own verse.[7] There is a minstrels' gallery in the banqueting hall in Old Gwernyfed (as the mansion is now called) at present, but the date at which it was installed is not known.

The sixteen verses of 'Welcome to Gwernyfed', as translated into English by Nesta Lloyd,[8] read:

> Listen to the welcome, fine lady, now I shall be so bold,
> Wife of a strong, young knight like a splendid Launcelot or Jason;
> This is the woman, fairest her form, that God himself has fashioned,
> Cheeks of wine no one had [like] her, she excels fair Dido;
> Welcome, now, lady, most able in Christendom, to Gwernyfed court.
>
> The name of the man who did not seek the [?Rine] of the just king
> Is Sir Harry Williams, handsome man, of the same strength as Samson;
> The name of the girl on whom his love was bestowed through marriage, true greetings,
> Is Eleanor, fairest living, of the lineage of Whitney of high breeding;
> Welcome, now, lady, most able in Christendom, to Gwernyfed court.
>
> This is a son of the great justice who is now the equal of Solomon,
> Highest on King James's Bench, Sir Dafydd Williams the just;
> There is no man at his side of greater sense than he,
> And everything here unfailingly surpasses everyone directly,
> Welcome, now, lady, most able in Christendom, to Gwernyfed court.
>
> Listen, lady of great fame, you can be content
> To see your estate in all places and your houses and white towers;
> God give graces, fair is the house of white-wash and clear glass,
> The sun rises on windows without shadows throughout the day;
> Welcome, now, lady, most able in Christendom, to Gwernyfed court.
>
> Hall, parlour, wine cellar and also an orderly kitchen;
> Buttery, pantry behind it, to feed a thousand men;
> Ale and beer for all men, wine and clear yellow bragget;
> Boiled and roast, I will not attempt to boast it, white [bread] and venison, great is the cost;
> Welcome, now, lady, most able in Christendom, to Gwernyfed court.
>
> And your tables are full of dishes, very sweet they taste;
> And your great venison pasties available warm at every hour,
> He has a gilded platter cover, greater than two earls,
> Every vessel on the table of the fine man himself are silver dishes;
> Welcome, now, lady, most able in Christendom, to Gwernyfed court.

And rooms, truly the finest within the land of Albion,
Of carved [? notable] work, God knows that they are magnificent;
And the beds and their appurtenances gold and silver in their hangings,
Excellent cambric, under them lordly princes could sleep,
Welcome, now, lady, most able in Christendom, to Gwernyfed court.

A brewery, a bake-house in addition, where drink is prepared for the servants,
And a place to bake white bread for strong and weak when they may come;
An excellent mill, a sty for the churn and with that, rooms for the poultry
And a rare house for the capons and a hunting-house for the hounds.
Welcome, now, lady, most able in Christendom, to Gwernyfed court.

And by the Court there is a garden of handsome plants, pure plants
And a mile of tidy, neat meadow, the finest under the Crown;
And on these there are flowers, numerous as the dew falling in the morning;
Princes could walk gracefully around the garden along each side
Welcome, now, lady, most able in Christendom, to Gwernyfed court.

And your fine orchards are the place which bears white apples,
Costards like white sugar, quince and red corslings;
And every tasty thing that can grow on a live tree
Fine is the smallest part of the flower, splendid is the root that fails nothing.
Welcome, now, lady, most able in Christendom, to Gwernyfed court.

Six or seven fish ponds without counting construction or greensward,
Until they draw into them the pure cold springs from every place;
Fine fish, these frequently play on each ripple,
Banks, repaired paving on which the privileged could walk.
Welcome, now, lady, most able in Christendom, to Gwernyfed court.

And your red falcons in straight enclosures and your fine, large hay meadows,
And your magnificent stables and your stallions grazing oats excessively;
A country which produces hay freely; fine indeed is the land where it is to be had;
And splendid barns and ?bins full of wheat to the doors.
Welcome, now, lady, most able in Christendom, to Gwernyfed court.

Nothing is missing except the park, do not worry that we do not see it.
We shall make it ready, shortly, full of young, brown animals;
Indeed, there is no man in the country better for a plump young animal,
The park of the squire, [a] conynger, that is preparation for fine fare.
Welcome, now, lady, most able in Christendom, to Gwernyfed court.

Let us give earnest thanks to God, we are quite content,
To have an aristocratic, gentle Welshwoman to listen to the complaints of the poor;
Hear now, dawn's flood, there is great welcome for you,
You are the head of Breconshire, long life to you, my knight;
Welcome, now, lady, most able in Christendom, to Gwernyfed court.

A thousand and six hundred exactly without sadness, was the age of Christ,
And five also, by the grace of God, when the fruitful marriage occurred;
Pretty lady, give me permission to say two words to you over our drink;
After receiving without fail, you must also be generous.
Welcome, now, lady, most able in Christendom, to Gwernyfed court.

God give to you the gift and grace and reputation which Tegau Eurfron received,
And from your soil, the flowers of our language, six or seven sons,
And each, fair his descent/form, as fortunate as the old man
Their grandfather, to whom God above gave most luck there ever was.
Welcome, now, lady, most able in Christendom, to Gwernyfed court.

Tegau Eurfron was a lady at the Court of King Arthur, discussed below.

From the poem and from the floor plan of the house, which was built in Elizabethan/
Jacobean style (Fig. 2.2) we learn that in 1605 the mansion at Gwernyfed had clear glass in
its windows, which many houses did not have at that time. The walls outside were white-
washed and thus white in colour. The mansion had a hall, parlour, kitchen, wine cellar and
other rooms. There probably was bardic exaggeration, or wishful thinking, in the claim
that there were enough facilities to feed a thousand men, with ale and beer for all of them!

The poem also tells us that there was plenty of food in the mansion, served in style on
'silver dishes'. Furthermore, the rooms were well furnished and the beds and their fittings
magnificent: 'gold and silver in their hangings/excellent cambric, under them lordly princes
could sleep'. The bard itemised the rooms where food and drink were stored and made – 'a
brewery, a bake-house' – and noted that there were also a mill, poultry houses, and kennels
for the hunting hounds. In fact, there was everything that a lady of the house could desire.

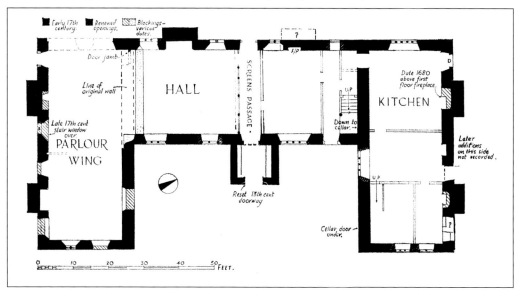

*Fig. 2.2. Ground-floor plan of Old Gwernyfed.*
*(By permission of the editor of* Brycheiniog)

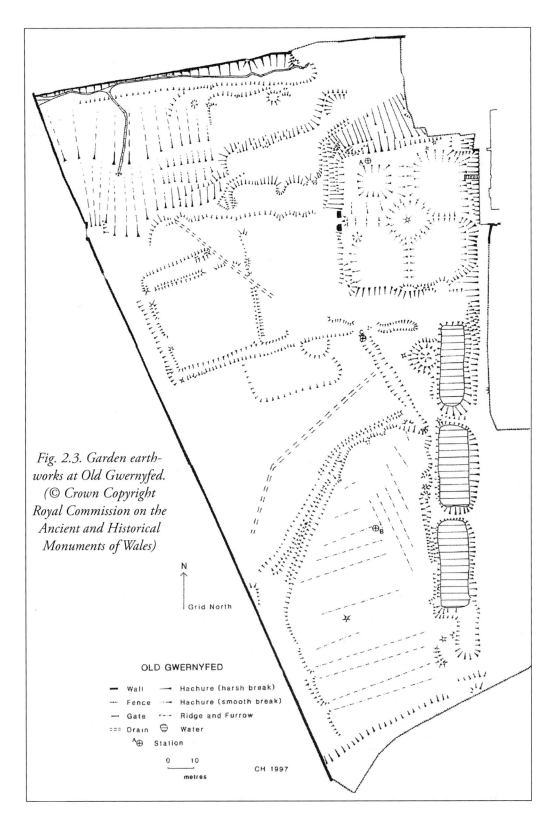

*Fig. 2.3. Garden earth-works at Old Gwernyfed. (© Crown Copyright Royal Commission on the Ancient and Historical Monuments of Wales)*

N
↑
| Grid North

OLD GWERNYFED

| — | Wall | — | Hachure (harsh break) |
| -- | Fence | -- | Hachure (smooth break) |
| — | Gate | --- | Ridge and Furrow |
| === | Drain | ⊖ | Water |
| A⊕ | Station | | |

0    10
metres          CH 1997

Outside the mansion there was a garden 'of handsome plants', lawn ('a mile of tidy, neat meadow, [and] flowers'. According to the bard the garden and lawn were fit for princes to walk around! Furthermore, there were orchards and fish ponds. Figure 2.3 is a surveyed drawing of the earthworks that still remain on the north-western side of the mansion and that may well be the remnants of the 'garden of handsome plants', although it is possible that they are of more recent origin.

The earthworks suggest that there was a formal Renaissance garden at Gwernyfed, in keeping with gardens that were then fashionable in the London and home-counties area, and at the Oxford and Cambridge colleges. Whoever designed them was obviously in touch with late 16th and early 17th centuries garden fashions, as a senior judge of the status of David Williams, or a cultured young lawyer such as his son Harry, who had studied at Oxford, should have been. The bride was therefore coming to a house and garden of taste, opulence and fashion (Fig. 2.4).

The fishponds, at a time when meat was not normally eaten on Fridays, which had been fast days under Roman Catholicism, were most important. Under King Henry VIII the established church had come under the authority of the monarch, but many of the features of Roman Catholicism were retained, at least as far as the populace were concerned. Friday, during the reign of Queen Elizabeth I (daughter of King Henry VIII) was commonly observed as a fast day, when meat should not be eaten. Fish, however, were regarded as acceptable food on Fridays and other fast days. Water for the fishponds was obtained from the brook that ran down off the Black Mountains and through the adjacent village of Velindre, and from springs on the slopes above and near Gwernyfed.

*Fig 2.4. The north-west face of Old Gwernyfed showing the terraces and other earthworks that are probably the remains of the Renaissance garden. The wing on the right of the mansion was damaged by fire in the late 18th century. (Photo by Colin Lewis)*

In his poem the bard assured the bride that her sporting needs, assuming she was interested in outdoor pursuits, would be provided for at Gwernyfed. In addition to kennels for hounds and magnificent stables for well-fed horses – 'horses grazing oats excessively' – there were also 'falcons in straight enclosures'. In other words the field sports that were fashionable in 1605 were well catered for.

Ben Johnson, the English playwright, had written in 1596 that if 'a man have not skill in the hawking and hunting languages nowadays, I'll not give a fig for him; they are more studied than the Greek or the Latin'. Queen Elizabeth had been a great follower of hawking and hunting, and when she was 66 years old a letter written by Sir Robert White stated that: 'Her majesty is well and excellently disposed to hunting for every second day she is on horseback, and continues the sport long'.[9]

Field sports continue to be important in the Gwernyfed area, where pheasant shoots abound in the opening decades of the 21st century, and where hounds still give tongue over the countryside, even if no longer hunting in traditional manner. In February 1924 the *Northern Daily Mail* reported that 'Hounds belonging to the Breconshire Hunt are missing in the Black Mountains. During a hunt near Talgarth a fox was discovered, and turning back towards Gwernyfed, made for the hills at a hot pace. For some miles the huntsmen kept up the chase but so hot was the run that the horsemen failed to keep up. The hounds … breasting the Black Mountains and disappearing in the direction of Abergavenny ... were last seen going in the direction of Cwmdu. The huntsman scoured the mountains yesterday and eventually found some of the hounds hungry and weary. It is believed the remainder of the pack is still wandering about [on the mountains].' How Eleanor and her husband would have enjoyed such a run!

Although bards, by tradition, glorified the achievements of those whose praises they sang, the Gwernyfed bard was honest enough to inform the bride that the park beyond the house had not yet been completed: 'Nothing is missing except the park'. He reassured her, however, that the park would be 'ready, shortly, full of young brown animals' (presumably rabbits). Indeed, her husband, and possibly his father, had done a great deal since David Williams bought Gwernyfed in 1600. In effect, a fashionable mansion now existed, complete with stables, kennels, hawk pens, fishponds and even a mill; gardens had been established, as had orchards and lawns. To complete all that work within five years was a major achievement.

From a marriage settlement of 1631 relating to Harry's son, Henry Williams the first baronet, and Anne Pie his bride, it is known that the park was eventually completed and rabbit warrens were built in it. A house between Velindre and Three Cocks is still named 'The Warren', indicating that rabbits were kept in its vicinity. Presumably Harry, being 'a coynger' (keeper of conies/rabbits), and his bride enjoyed many plump young rabbits from their warren in the years after their wedding in 1605. Harry is also known to have stocked the park with deer, since they are also listed in the 1631 marriage settlement. After all, as the bard told his listeners: 'great venison pasties [were] available warm at every hour' at Gwernyfed, and Harry had to ensure the availability of a source of venison, even if only to avoid incurring future bardic wrath!

Bards, of course, may exaggerate. They may also be a little naughty! The composer of the welcome poem was no exception, for he was naughty, but in a refined way. In verse 16 he prayed that God would give the bride the gift and grace and reputation of [in the Welsh original] *teg eirffron*. These words were a jumble of letters that could be interpreted as the name *Tegau Eurfron*. She was the only lady at the Court of King Arthur who is supposed to have passed 'a chastity test when a testing talisman of a mantle or cloak was sent to the court. The property of the mantle was that it would completely cover any chaste wife, but it would be revealingly short on an unfaithful lady'![10] The well-oiled gentlemen at the feast appreciated this quip, no doubt, (it came in the last verse by when there had been plenty of time for lubrication), but whether the ladies laughed as well is less certain!

Gwernyfed was not only a large and fashionable mansion by 1605, but it was also a statement of the status of Sir David Williams and his family in society. As Dafydd Johnston has written: 'It was customary for the wealthy landed gentry of the later Middle Ages to build themselves fine houses as imposing symbols of their social status.'[11] He added that these houses: 'served as focal points for the surrounding communities'. Sir David and his son, no matter which of them paid for the mansion, were obviously wealthy, and Gwernyfed, with its great hall, parlour wing and kitchen, let alone its stables, kennels, hawk pens, gardens, fishponds and orchards, was a visible statement of wealth and status. Eleanor was fortunate to be able to live in such an impressive place!

*Fig 2.5. The entrance porch at Old Gwernyfed. The archway is thought to date to the 13th century and to formerly have been part of the church in Velindre or of some other local church. (Photo by Colin Lewis)*

Adding to the status of the mansion is the entrance porch with its 13th-century arch (Fig. 2.5) which is thought to have been obtained from the now demolished Velindre church. This was a chapel of Glasbury church and the present Village Hall has been built on its site. Whether this porch was part of the mansion when Eleanor came there, or whether it was added later, is unknown. Baptisms, weddings and burials continued to take place at Velindre Chapel (i.e. the church) down to 1695, as shown by the registers of Glasbury, and the arch may have been removed to Old Gwernyfed when the church was closed.

13

The idea that mansions such as Gwernyfed formed 'focal points for the surrounding communities' is evidenced by the bard's admonition to the bride: that she 'listen to the complaints of the poor', and that she 'must be generous'. The whole idea that the bard was trying to convey was that Gwernyfed was the centre of the local community, where rich and poor came not only as visitors but as supplicants and as traditional members of what was essentially a feudal society. In a sense both rich and poor were part of Gwernyfed and Gwernyfed was part of them. Sir David, her father-in-law, was indeed generous. In his will, for example, he left money not only to repair Glasbury Bridge, (which was a vital transport link in the region), and maintain local roads, but also to provide bread for the poor of Aberllynfi and Velindre, and money for meat, drink and clothing for 'the distressed poor near Gwernyfed'.[12]

The local community included farmers, their families and workers, craftsmen, millers, woodsmen, tailors, blacksmiths and many others, plus clergy and gentry from nearby areas. Some of the farmers lived in dwellings that dated back to the 16th century or even earlier. Newcourt Farm, for example, located about half-a-mile east of Gwernyfed mansion, is an extended form of the traditional Welsh long-house[13] and dates back to at least the late 16th century with additions, including a remarkable wooden staircase, that were added in the mid-17th century when the Williams family were at Gwernyfed.[14] Many labourers and squatters, however, must have lived in miserable cottages, such as Eurwyn William depicts in his book on *The Welsh Cottage*.

The traditional hospitality of Welsh society, where hospitality was extended to all and where even the poorest could expect to be fed, was reflected by the bard with the words: 'receiving without fail', with the reminder about being generous. As G.R. Hibbard stated in his article entitled 'The country house poem of the seventeenth century',[15] the landlord's mansion 'is the embodiment of a natural bond between lord and tenant'.

Saunders Lewis, in writing about the great Welsh bard Dafydd Nanmor (*c*.1445-90) and his vision of life,[16] maintained, like Hibbard, that a mansion was 'the quintessence of a noble civilization, and that this is the masterpiece of mankind, ... the great principle of conservatism and nobility, the communion of the generations, with the House as a dignified symbol of the unbroken sacrament'. Gwernyfed remained the centre 'of the unbroken sacrament' as

*Fig. 2.6 The Aberllynfi font, dated 1635, that is now used in St Peter's Church, Glasbury. (Photo by Colin Lewis)*

long as it was the home of the landlord and open to local society. Once the male line of Sir David Williams' family was broken, as it was in 1675 when the heiress married into a different Williams' family, Gwernyfed's role as centre of society in the area was in jeopardy.

There is some evidence that Sir Henry acquired the adjacent estate of Llangoed, near Llyswen and north-west of Gwernyfed, in 1632. An arch over a doorway at Llangoed Castle bears the date 1632 while an outer arch of the porch carries the arms of Einion Sais and the inscription SIR H.W. KNIGHT GLORIAM DEO CANO.[17] Clough Williams-Ellis (1883-1978), the renowned architect, supplied drawings in the early 1900s for alterations and additions to Llangoed and its outbuildings and major alterations were subsequently undertaken, obscuring much of the 'original' buildings.

In 1635, the year before Sir Harry died, he and Eleanor donated an octagonal stone font to Aberllynfi church. Among the carvings on the font is the outline of a shield bearing the letter W above the letters SHE. Beneath the initials is the date: 1635. The W obviously stands for Williams while the S and H presumably represent 'Sir Henry' (or Harry as Sir Henry was commonly called) and the E his wife 'Eleanor'. This font is now located in St Peter's Church in Glasbury and continues to serve its original purpose (Fig. 2.6).

Under Sir Harry's leadership an appreciable amount of building took place on the Gwernyfed estate. The building that is Three Cocks Hotel, for example, dates to the early 17th century and may have been built in Sir Harry's era (Fig. 2.7). It became a coaching inn, with stables on the opposite side of the main road from Brecon to Hay that are now a

*Fig. 2.7 The Three Cocks Hotel. Notice the arms of Einion Sais: three red cocks divided by a red chevron, on the gables of the hotel. (From a watercolour by A.R. Quinton, courtesy of the owner of the painting: Mrs Windham)*

Fig. 2.8 The remains of Aberllynfi church, photographed in 2016. (Photo by Marijke Lewis)

Fig. 2.9 Edward Lhuyd's drawing of the tomb of Sir Harry Williams that was erected in Aberllynfi church. (MS Rawl.C.920, fol.3r. Reproduced by permission of The Bodleian Library, University of Oxford)

restaurant. A lane from the main road led to Aberllynfi village green. The house at the end of the green is reputed to have been The Rectory, although, since Aberllynfi church was on the opposite side of the brook and served by clergy from Glasbury, that is unlikely.

After his death in 1636 Sir Harry and his wife were remembered by a notable stone memorial in Aberllynfi church, which also depicts their four sons and two daughters. The church was located near what are now the remnant earthworks of a castle above the confluence of Tregoyd Brook with the flood plain of the Llynfi and Wye rivers. Unfortunately the church became redundant in the 1750s after the death of Mary Howarth, the remarried widow of another Henry Williams, as described in the next chapter. The church is now no more than a ruin (Fig. 2.8).

Nothing remains of Sir Harry's tomb except a drawing by Edward Lhuyd that is housed in the Bodleian Library at Oxford University (Fig. 2.9). When Theophilus Jones' *History of Brecknockshire* was first published, in 1800, it stated that in Aberllynfi church there were 'a few mutilated monuments upon the Williams' of Gwernyfed and Llangoed, one is an effigy of a person in judicial robes, but lacking the head'. Vandalism is not a new phenomenon!

Following Sir Harry's death, Gwernyfed passed to his eldest son, Sir Henry Williams (1607-1656). He was created a baronet in 1644 and briefly hosted King Charles I at Gwernyfed as the latter fled after the Battle of Naseby in 1645. The chair on which it was said that the king sat for a meal was displayed in the banqueting hall at Old Gwernyfed until the 1950s. In 1647 there was a disagreement over the annuity supposed, under Sir Harry's will, to be paid to Eleanor, and this culminated in a Chancery suit.

On the death of Henry, the first baronet, he was succeeded by yet another Henry Williams, the second baronet (1635-1666), who married Abigail Wightwick. Her father was a member of the Inner Temple. They had two sons who died without male issue, and a daughter, Elizabeth (1662-1705), who became heiress to the Gwernyfed estate.

Henry and Abigail lived through turbulent times during which Oliver Cromwell and his supporters were responsible for the execution of King Charles I in 1649. This was followed by the republican Commonwealth Period (1649-1660) in which Oliver Cromwell (1599-1658) became Lord Protector until his death in 1658. His son, who then led the country, proved far less effective a leader than his father. In 1660 an army officer, General Monck, supported by sufficient troops, ensured that Charles' son, Charles II, was crowned king at the Restoration of the Monarchy.

During the Cromwellian period Puritan feelings ran high, and many churches were vandalised with rood screens demolished, statues and crosses destroyed, and churches generally neglected. Rood screens were divisions, sometimes surmounted by a loft wide enough to walk on, with a cross (rood) on top of the screen or walkway. These screens divided the chancel of a church, which was the preserve of the priests, from the nave, which is where the congregation were accommodated.

The rood screen in the Priory Church (now the cathedral) in Brecon was renowned throughout Wales prior to the Cromwellian period, and was a focus for pilgrims from far and wide until it was destroyed. Nearer Gwernyfed, at Llanelieu, a crude wooden rood screen still exists (Fig. 2.10). The outline of the cross (rood) still exists as a shadow outlined by paintwork on the timbers above the rood loft. Elyned, the author of *A Victorian*

*Fig. 2.10 The wooden rood screen that still survives in Llanelieu church.
The bell cote of that church houses another treasure: a late 12th- or early 13th-century bell.
(Photo by Colin Lewis)*

*Childhood*, probably rode past that church on many occasions, especially as she journeyed to and from her home to the adjoining settlement of Talgarth via Velindre and Common Bychan, the open common above Velindre.

Llanelieu, isolated and tucked away in the Ellwye valley above Talgarth, at the foot of the Black Mountains, obviously escaped serious attention by the Cromwellians. They also seem to have overlooked the church in Llanfilo, west of Talgarth, where a beautiful rood screen and loft with fine carvings also survives. This screen and loft was restored in the early 20th century.

Under the Cromwellians many clergy of the established church were ejected from their livings, including Alexander Griffiths, vicar of Glasbury. Griffiths was a member of the Griffiths family of Y Gaer in the parish of Llowes. He was educated at Hart Hall in the University of Oxford before being instituted as Vicar of Glasbury in 1639. In June 1650 he was ejected from his parish and succeeded by various un-ordained people 'accounted among us as vicar[s]'.[18] Following the Restoration of the Monarchy in 1660 Alexander Griffiths resumed his duties as rightful vicar of Glasbury.

Glasbury church, located on the flood plain of the Rivers Wye and Llynfi, had been badly damaged by flood waters and presumably suffered from lack of maintenance during the Cromwellian period. Griffiths and many of his parishioners believed that rather than repair the church, a new church should be built on higher ground, above the flood plain. Consequently they petitioned the bishop of St David's, in which diocese Glasbury was then located, requesting permission to salvage material from the damaged church 'towards the building of another'. The petition was signed by Alexander Griffiths (vicar of Glasbury), Henry Williams (the second baronet),[19] Milburn Williams, and nearly a hundred parishioners.[20]

Following the success of the petition, Sir Henry gave a site for the new church on ground above flood level beside the road from Glasbury to Brecon and approximately half way between the villages of Glasbury and Aberllynfi/Three Cocks. The site lay under the common known as Coed y Bolin and was thereafter known as Clas (Church) dan Coed y Bolin. (The modern spelling of Bolin substitutes an e for an i). The church was completed by 1664 and was consecrated by the bishop of St David's the following year. Before the consecration ceremony the bishop asked Sir Henry to 'digg a turfe, and give it into the B'pp's gowne'. Sir Henry then said: '… by this turfe I resigne upp all my interest in this circuit of ground, to be a buringe-place for ever for the dead of this parishe of Glasebury'. The bishop then consecrated the ground '… to be a resting place for the bodyes of those who shal be buried here, until the last day of doome'.[21]

The first burial took place on 30 July 1665 and the churchyard is still in use. As shall be seen later, the author of *A Victorian Childhood* walked through that churchyard on many occasions as she went to and from church. The church that she attended, however, was the Victorian successor to that dedicated by the bishop in 1665. The 1665 church consisted of 'a chancel, a nave, and a low square tower, having sloping pyramidal roof covered, like the rest of the edifice, with tiles and surmounted by a weather-vane … The principal entrance was in the southern wall of the nave, near the tower, and protected by a porch having stone benches, and a wooden gate' (Fig. 2.11).[22]

*Fig. 2.11 Probable appearance of St Peter's Church, Glasbury, consecrated in 1665.
A pen and ink reconstruction by Dr M.A.V. Gill based on written description of the building,
depiction on an estate map of the 1720s and other evidence.*

In 1675 Sir Henry's daughter and heiress, Elizabeth, married Sir Edward Williams (1659-1721) of the Williams family of Talyllyn.[23] His father, Sir Thomas Williams (*c*.1621-1712)[24] was chemical physician to King Charles II. Sir Edward found that the Gwernyfed estate was worth only about £700 per annum and was greatly encumbered, so his heiress was not a very successful catch financially! In 1680, if a date on a fireplace inside the mansion is not misleading, alterations took place to the house, perhaps to make it more suitable than formerly for Elizabeth and her husband to live in.[25] In 1698 Edward Lhuyd visited the area and reported that, in Aberllynfi parish, there was 'one village consisting of abt 9 houses', but he did not comment on Gwernyfed itself. The village, presumably, was what is now named 'Three Cocks'.

# 3   GWERNYFED IN THE 18TH CENTURY

Following the death of Sir Henry Williams, the second baronet, in 1666, and the deaths of his two sons without male issue, Gwernyfed passed to his daughter, Elizabeth Williams. As already mentioned, in July 1675 she married Edward Williams (1659-1721), of the Talyllyn family of Williams. Her groom was no more than 17 and she was probably only 14, and the marriage was held by licence. Edward may not have realised, when he married her, that the Gwernyfed estate produced so little money – only about £700 per annum – and was heavily encumbered. He was still trying to clear his father-in-law's debts in 1703, when he obtained an Act for that purpose.[1]

Edward, who had been knighted previously, entered parliament at a by-election in 1697, but was granted leave of absence the following year. He was not elected as a Member of Parliament again until 1705, the year his wife, Elizabeth, died. During the intervening period he had been greatly concerned with clearing his debts. As far as is known Sir Edward lived at Gwernyfed until his death in 1721. He was buried in the churchyard at Aberllynfi, as his father had been in 1712.

*Fig. 3.1  The founder's mark of Henry Williams on a bell that he cast in 1693 for the church at Mansell Gamage in Herefordshire. (Photo by Colin Lewis)*

The Pipton Forge, located in the parish of Aberllynfi on the Gwernyfed estate and close to the small settlement of Pipton, was an industrial enterprise on Sir Edward's estate. In the second decade of the 18th century the forge was operated by Henry Williams, best known as 'The Glasbury bellfounder'.[2] There is no certain evidence that the bellfounder was related to his landlord's family. Henry Williams the bellfounder is known to have cast bells between 1677 and 1719, and most of them seem to have been cast for churches or people associated with the Gwernyfed estate.

Williams' first known bell was cast in 1677 for Llanwnog in Cardiganshire, which was, for a while, a distant and isolated part of the Gwernyfed estate. On that bell he cast the triumphant inscription: HENRICVS WILLIAMS ME FECIT ANNO DOMINI 1677 GLORIA SIT DEO.

*Fig. 3.2 Forge Cottage, Aberllynfi, as it was in the 1950s. Henry Williams the bell founder probably lived in this house, which is now a ruin, in his latter days. The apparent remnants of the forge are located upstream of the cottage, near the confluence of the Velindre Brook with the River Llynfi. (Reproduced courtesy of Talgarth Historical Society: Jack Pettican Collection)*

Many of Henry's bells carry his founder's mark of a bell within a pair of callipers surmounted by his initials with a raised dot below each initial and below the clapper of the bell. Callipers were used by bell founders when they were designing and laying-out the profiles of bells, so his mark effectively summarised and advertised Williams' skill (Fig. 3.1). Williams' last known bell was cast in 1719 and he died in 1722 leaving a daughter and a grandson, but no known son.

The bellfounder's will, dated 22 May 1721, shows that he then held leasehold lands from Sir Edward Wms of Gwernevett and occupied the Pipton Forge and presumably lived in Forge Cottage (Fig. 3.2). Henry Williams died on 8 March 1722 and, according to Dawson,[3] the forge was let by Sir Edward's successor, another Henry Williams, to new tenants: Benjamin Tanner (an 'ironmonger' of Brecon) and Richard Wellington (a 'gentleman' of Hay). Wellington lived in Hay Castle and was Sheriff of Breconshire in 1726. The bellfounder was buried in the churchyard of St Peter's, Glasbury. His abiding memorials are the bells he cast, especially, the ring of five bells he cast, tuned and hung for ringing at St Michael's church, Clyro, in 1708.

The Pipton Forge was operated throughout the remainder of the 1720s by Tanner and Wellington in conjunction with their forge and furnace at the Brecon Ironworks, which supplied pig iron to the Pipton Forge. Charcoal, then used to heat forges, requires plentiful supplies of wood for its production and it was cheaper to locate forges near woodland sources of charcoal production, due to costs of transportation, (wood being bulky and costly to transport), rather than near the sources of iron ore and of the limestone that was used in the smelting process. Early forges and furnaces were thus located in essentially rural areas. Consequently, by the late 1600s if not before, there was an industrial aspect to the Gwernyfed estate. Some 30 per cent of the iron output of south Wales in the 1720s came from the Brecon Ironworks and the Pipton Forge.[4]

Sir Edward died on 28 July 1721, and was buried at Aberllynfi, as his father had been in 1712. Following Sir Edward's death he was briefly succeeded by his son, the Henry who entered into the Indenture with Tanner and Wellington as described above. Henry married Mary Walbeoffe of Llanhamlach in the Usk valley downstream of Brecon, but died without issue in 1723. Mary remarried in the year her husband died, and retained a term for life on the Gwernyfed estate and on Aberllynfi church.

Mary's new husband, Sir Humphrey Howarth (1684-1755),[5] had properties at Cabalfa near the village of Clyro and at Maesllwch in Glasbury and was Member of Parliament for the County of Radnor (1722-1755). In 1738 he was also Governor of Barbados. Unfortunately Sir Humphrey had financial problems and mortgaged Maesllwch. The mortgage was foreclosed 'and the demesne afterwards purchased by Walter Wilkins'. The Wilkins family, who had struck rich in India and then become bankers in Brecon, subsequently obtained a royal licence to change their surname to De Winton, and that family still live at what is now known as Maesllwch Castle. Mary died in 1742. Following Mary's death Aberllynfi church, where services had been taken by clergy from Glasbury for many years, was closed.

Henry was succeeded by his brother, David, who died in 1740. From an unknown date after Sir Edward's death in 1721 the Talyllyn Williams family seem to have preferred to reside at Llangoed, near Llyswen, rather than at Gwernyfed itself. This is evidenced by a document of 1769 by 'Sir Edward Williams, bart [1728-1804], of Langoid Castle and other gentlemen of co. Brec.'.[6] Sir Edward's address in modern spelling is clearly Llangoed.

As a result Old Gwernyfed, as it is now called, eventually became a tenanted farmhouse with its associated farm buildings, rather than a mansion that was the centre of the estate and the home of the landlord and his family. This phase in the history of the mansion is reflected by Thomas Perks' contribution to this book – Chapter 6, *Life at Gwernyfed in the 1860s* – which, describing conditions in the pre-internal combustion, gas and electrical eras, was probably little different from life on that farm in the second half of the 18th century.

Sir David was succeeded for a very brief period by his son, another Sir Henry, who died, unmarried, in 1741. Sir David's second son, Sir Edward (1728-1804), then succeeded. Sir Edward had a son (also named Edward) who predeceased him in 1799 and a daughter, Mary, who became the heiress.

During the 1700s, if not before, there was much change in the local cultural landscape. The River Wye, for example, proved difficult to bridge at Glasbury due to sudden violent floods and at least two bridges were destroyed in the 1700s, one in 1738/9 and another in February 1795. On 11 February 1795 there was a 'very sudden thaw after the long frost in the beginning of 1795', and 'a torrent of ice' came down the river and destroyed all the

*Fig. 3.3  Glasbury Bridge, built in 1777 and destroyed by the great flood*
*of 11 February 1795. (From a sketch by Ursula Cooper from an engraving*
*of an illustration in Samuel Ireland's* Picturesque Views on the River Wye *of 1797)*

*Fig. 3.4  William Edwards (1719-*
*1789) designer and builder of*
*Glasbury bridge, 1777.*
*(From a miniature portrait*
*by Thomas Hill [Junior])*

arches of Glasbury bridge (Fig. 3.3). The flood also destroyed Hay and Whitney bridges and seriously damaged others. At Hampton Bishop, downstream of Hereford, 'the water rose six feet in half an hour'.[7]

The bridge destroyed in 1795 had been designed and built by William Edwards (1719-1789) of Caerphilly (Fig. 3.4). Edwards had made his reputation by designing and building a single-arch bridge over the River Taff at Pontypridd in 1756. He subsequently built bridges across the Usk, Tawe, Aman, Tywi and Afon before working on Glasbury bridge.[8] Ferry boats, such as those depicted in Fig. 3.3, continued in use at Glasbury until at least the 1890s.

There were, however, many other changes to the cultural landscape in the late 17th and the 18th centuries. Sir Edward Williams (1728-1804), like other landlords elsewhere at that time in Britain and Ireland, employed surveyors to map his estate (as already seen on Fig. 2.1) and even to show the location of the dwellings of his tenants adjacent to common land (Fig. 3.5). The old manorial field system, where it still existed, was replaced with rigidly organised and surveyed fields, bounded by hedges and, in many cases, by ditches. These ditches helped drain the land.

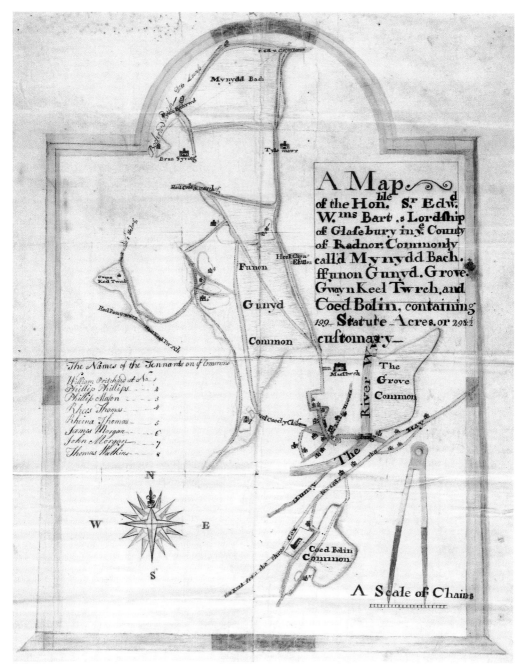

*Fig. 3.5 A map dated 1750 showing the dwellings of tenants on Sir Edward Williams' commons around Glasbury. (By permission of Llyfrgell Genedlaethol Cymru / The National Library of Wales, Gwernyfed Estate Records)*

*Fig. 3.6 Geometrically organised fields on the slopes of Mynydd Troed, near Talgarth, probably reflect planned reorganisation of the landscape during the Agrarian Revolution of the 17th and 18th centuries. (Photographed in April 2016)*

Hedges were normally planted on earthen banks using hawthorn, blackthorn or similar plants which, being thorny, would be a barrier to livestock when properly grown and laid. Hazel was also commonly used as a hedge plant. The saplings, when about 12 feet high, were partially cut near their bases and then woven (or 'laid') between stakes driven into the hedge bank at one to two yard intervals, forming a stock-proof hedge. Long shoots of hazel, cut from the hedging plants, were then placed on top of the hedge, parallel to the ground, and were woven between the tops of the stakes. They were then forced down on to the sloping saplings to bind them tightly together.

Land within fields was increasingly drained with clay pipes laid in trenches and covered with gravel or other pervious material. These pipes eventually drained into streams or into hedge ditches. Fencing, ditching, bank making, planting, hedge-laying and draining must have employed much manual labour, and transformed the landscape into a geometrical pattern of fields (Fig. 3.6).

During Sir Edward's land-lordship a thriving wool stapling industry existed on the Gwernyfed estate, based at Treble Hill in Glasbury and owned by John Morgan (1748-1824) and his successors.[9] The Morgan family operated their business in a warehouse located between the Georgian residence at Treble Hill (Fig. 3.7) and what was later to become Glasbury Railway Station. They bought wool from farmers in mid-Wales and elsewhere, transported it to the Treble Hill warehouse where it was sorted and graded, and then sold it, particularly to local woollen mills and to mills in Yorkshire.

*Fig. 3.7 Treble Hill, the former home of John Morgan (1748-1824), wool stapler.
(Photographed in February 2016 by Marijke Lewis)*

Woollen and grain mills were widespread in much of Wales, as elsewhere, wherever there was an adequate source of running water to drive mill wheels. The Welsh name '*Pandy*', common in the Marches, means 'woollen mill'. There were at least two grain mills active on the Tregoyd Brook until the early 20th century – at Tregoyd Mill and at Three Cocks. The name of the village near Old Gwernyfed – Velindre – translates from the Welsh as 'Mill Town'.

The wool stapling business thrived under successive generations of the Morgan family until, in 1839, some of the banks in Yorkshire failed. That meant that some Yorkshire woollen millers who had bought wool from the Morgans were unable to pay for it. Nevertheless, the Morgan wool staplers still had to pay for the wool that they had purchased, and that proved a disaster for at least one member of the family. Thomas Morgan (1796-1847) had been a highly respected member of local society and one of the two churchwardens of Glasbury in 1838 when the present St Peter's church with its six bells was opened.[10] Thomas lost almost all his assets in clearing his debts, and had to leave the area and take a job in Abergavenny, running The Angel Hotel. His two brothers, who were also wool staplers, were fortunately less affected and managed to remain in Glasbury, at Treble Hill and at Ty'r Uched, near Treble Hill.

Thomas and his wife, Mary Anne née Vaughan (died 1840), had nine sons, one of whom, Walter Vaughan Morgan (1831-1916), became Lord Mayor of London in 1905. Walter was to donate the stained glass window in memory of his parents that is in Brecon cathedral. He and his surviving brothers also donated two bells to complete the octave at Glasbury.

The Treble Hill warehouse was eventually transformed into a set of three cottages and when the railway was extended from Hereford to Glasbury in the 1860s, a number of them were let to railway employees.[11] Long before then ownership of the Gwernyfed estate had passed, through marriage, to the Wood family.

For many years Sir Edward Williams had been plagued by financial problems and had borrowed extensively against the security of his estate. By 1790 he owed at least £24,000, with interest at 5%. By 1791 'Sir Edward had decamped from Llangoed and taken up residence at Clifton Wood, near Bristol'.[12] Perhaps he thought the atmosphere at Clifton more suitable for his eyes, which had latterly become sore, than that at Llangoed.

In 1795 Sir Edward, who had to cope with a somewhat feckless and argumentative son also named Edward, tried to sell the Gwernyfed estate. The estate included Llangoed itself and stretched from valleys on the south side of the Black Mountains to the Epynt, from Cathedine to the parish of Hay, and into Llanstephan in Radnorshire, though did not include every property in those areas. At that time, with much unrest in France and consequent uncertainty at home, selling proved difficult, but in 1796 he struck a deal with John Macnamara, 'a wealthy London gentleman'. The deal was complicated and involved the outright sale of that part of the estate 'not owned or controlled by trustees' for 'a capital sum of £39,000, with a payment of £8,000 to Mary Wood', as well as two annuities. Other parts of the estate were to be leased to Macnamara 'for an annual rent of £1,600' on 'a lease for three lives'. There were many other clauses, and lengthy and tortuous law suits followed as to which parts of the estate had been sold, which leased and which retained, which took some 30 years to resolve as outlined in the next chapter.[13]

When Sir Edward died in 1804, he had been predeceased by his only son – Major Edward Williams – who had died in 1799. Sir Edward's only daughter, Mary Williams, was therefore heiress to the Gwernyfed estate. She had married Thomas I Wood of Littleton, Middlesex, in June 1776.

# 4   Gwernyfed and the Wood family

The Woods had risen to prominence in the mid-17th century when Edward Wood, 'citizen and grocer of London', established his seat at Littleton, which was then in Middlesex (Fig. 4.1).[1]

The Woods were substantial landowners. They had purchased the Middleham estate in Yorkshire in the 17th century and the marriage of Thomas I Wood (1748-1835) and Mary Williams (1752-1820) on 12 June 1776 added the Gwernyfed estate to their portfolio. They

*Fig. 4.1 Littleton Park House, built by Edward Wood in the mid-17th century, burnt in December 1874, restored and now part of Shepperton Studios. (Photo courtesy of Shepperton Studios)*

continued to live mainly at Littleton until the mansion was destroyed by fire in December 1874. After the fire, between 1877 and 1880, Colonel Thomas IV Wood (1853-1933), father of Elyned, the author of Chapter 5 of this book, built a new house in Jacobean style in the parkland at Gwernyfed. This mansion, which replaced an older three-storeyed house, shown as painted white in the only picture known of it, was named Gwernyfed Park.

Thomas I, Mary's husband, had shares in the English East India Company as well as other assets. He therefore seems to have had a sound financial base from which to operate. When problems arose over what had, or had not been sold or leased by Mary's father to John Macnamara, who proved litigious, Thomas was not frightened to protect his new interests.

There followed a difficult period in which, in 1801, Macnamara had trees felled on the estate which the Woods maintained he had no right to do. In 1802 the Woods obtained an injunction preventing Macnamara from felling trees near Gwernyfed mansion. They noted that the mansion 'was surrounded by many trees which provided both ornament and shelter' and argued that Macnamara and his servants were about 'to fell every tree with a girth of six inches and above. Even immature trees were to be cut.'[2]

In 1807, after Macnamara began an action relating to the lease to him of certain areas of land, the Woods countered that 'the lands which Macnamara was asking to have for £1,600 per annum had actually been let for nearly £2,000 in 1796'. Legalities dragged on and eventually Thomas II Wood (1777-1860) 'was largely driving the litigation on behalf of his father and mother'.[3]

John Macnamara died in May 1818 when he was 63, while litigation still continued. Eventually, in 1828, his son, Arthur, and the Woods came to an agreement and the Llangoed estate was split in two. The litigation had proved expensive; between 1796 and 1828 Thomas I Wood's lawyers invoiced him for over £1,600, the equivalent of about £120,000 at 2016 values.

When Thomas II succeeded his father in 1835 he inherited an estimated £88,000.[4] His parents, Thomas I and Mary, had ensured that their son was well educated, attending Harrow from 1788 until 1795 before going up to Oriel College, Oxford in 1796. Perhaps his parents were also instrumental in his advantageous marriage to Lady Caroline Stewart (1781-1865) in December 1801 (Table 1).

The Stewarts hailed from Londonderry in the north of Ireland where Lady Caroline's paternal grandfather, Alexander Stewart, had been an alderman in 1760. Alexander's wife, Mary Cowan, was the sister and heiress of Robert Cowan: 'who gained great wealth as Governor of Bombay from 1729 to 1737'.[5] Consequently much of the Stewart family wealth came through Robert Cowan via the marriage of Mary and Alexander.

Lady Caroline's father, Robert Stewart (1739-1821), was Alexander's second son and entered the linen trading business in Dublin. After the death of his elder brother, Robert moved back to Ulster to help with family properties there. He became active in politics and in 1771 was elected MP for Down in the Irish House of Commons. He lost that seat in 1783 but was appointed to the Irish Privy Council. In 1799 the Bill for an Act of Union between Britain and Ireland was rejected by the Irish Parliament, but Stewart campaigned for it to be re-introduced. In 1801 both countries were united.

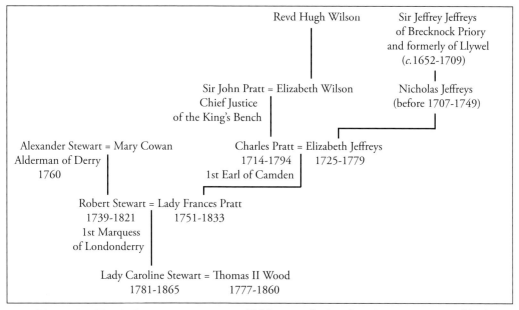

Revd Hugh Wilson

Sir Jeffrey Jeffreys
of Brecknock Priory
and formerly of Llywel
(*c.*1652-1709)

Nicholas Jeffreys
(before 1707-1749)

Sir John Pratt = Elizabeth Wilson
Chief Justice
of the King's Bench

Alexander Stewart = Mary Cowan
Alderman of Derry
1760

Charles Pratt = Elizabeth Jeffreys
1714-1794    1725-1779
1st Earl of Camden

Robert Stewart = Lady Frances Pratt
1739-1821        1751-1833
1st Marquess
of Londonderry

Lady Caroline Stewart = Thomas II Wood
1781-1865                 1777-1860

*Table 1 Lady Caroline Stewart's ancestral links to the Jeffreys family of Breconshire that predated her marriage to Thomas Wood (1777-1860).*

*Fig. 4.2 Robert Stewart,*
*1st Marquess of Londonderry,*
*by William Daniell, after George Dance.*
*Stewart (1739-1821) was father of*
*Lady Caroline Stewart (1781-1865),*
*who married Thomas Wood (1777-1860)*
*in 1801. (© National Portrait Gallery,*
*London)*

Robert's first wife was Lady Sarah Frances Seymour-Conway (1747-70). His second wife, whom he married in 1775, the mother of Lady Caroline, was Lady Frances Pratt (1751-1833): she was of good Welsh stock on her maternal line. Perhaps it was partly through her influence that Stewart was created Marquess of Londonderry in 1816 (Fig. 4.2).

Lady Frances was daughter of Charles Pratt (1714-94) and Elizabeth Jeffreys (1725-79). Charles, who was of a Devonshire family, was created 1st Earl of Camden in 1765 and his political career included the posts of Attorney-General and Lord Chancellor. Pratt made money out of his legal practice and out of property development in the London area (Camden Town) although much of his wealth is said to have been derived from his second wife, Elizabeth Jeffreys.

Elizabeth Jeffreys was sole heir of her father, Nicholas Jeffreys (before 1707 until 1749). Nicholas was an heir of his father, Sir Jeffrey Jeffreys (*c.*1652-1709) of Brecknock Priory and formerly of Llywel. Sir Jeffrey and his brother had been educated at the expense of their uncle, John Jeffreys, a tobacco merchant and Alderman of London. On John's death his estate, believed to be worth about £300,000, was divided between the brothers.

Jeffrey used at least some of his share to purchase Brecknock Priory and in 1690 became local MP. He had major international business interests and was 'particularly successful in the West Indian slave trade'.[6] He became English agent for the Leeward Islands and informally for Virginia. He also traded in Spain, North Africa, and the Baltic and had shares in the English East India Company. When he died, in 1709, he left a fortune worth about £140,000.

The Jeffreys were generally considered to be among the more affluent of Breconshire families. There was thus a link between the Stewarts and Breconshire, and therefore with members of the Gwernyfed estate, long before Thomas II married Lady Caroline Stewart in 1801.

Subsequent to his marriage in 1801, Thomas II (Fig. 4.3) took a major interest in politics and was elected Member of Parliament for Breconshire in 1806. He held the seat until 1847. Unlike a previous owner of the Gwernyfed estate, Sir Henry (Harry) Williams (1579/80-1636), who was a supporter of Welsh culture, a Welsh speaker, and even wrote his own poetry (though this in English), Wood maintained in 1820 that the widespread use of the Welsh language was 'evidence of the Principality's backwardness'. Wood argued that the end of the language was nigh. These utterances brought on him considerable wrath, and the MP for Pembroke Boroughs drew attention to Wood's non-residence in Wales and questioned his right to speak as a Welshman.

Four years earlier, in 1816, Wood chaired a meeting of subscribers to Glasbury National School, which opened that year at Coed y Bolen, on the hill above St Peter's Church (Fig. 4.4). Welsh was not on the curriculum. The cost of building the schoolroom was largely met by Miss Bridget Hughes of Glasbury House, who contributed £211 17s 6d, Wood subscribed five guineas (£5 5s) towards

*Fig. 4.3 Thomas II Wood (1777-1860).*
*(From a painting by the school of William Owen*
*[1769-1825] c.1810, reference BRCNM 2003.1.1,*
*by permission of the*
*Brecknock Museum and Art Gallery)*

*Fig. 4.4 Glasbury school, opened in 1816 and closed in 2012. The headmaster's house is in the centre of the picture, the more recent infants school room projects to the left with the roof of the original schoolroom rising just beyond it. The canteen with its flat roof is to the far left, the toilet block to the right. (Photo by Colin Lewis, 2016)*

the school and his wife, Lady Caroline, did likewise. Walter Wilkins, Esq., MP, who has already entered this story by lending money to Sir Edward Williams, contributed a similar amount, as did Sir Charles Morgan, Bt., MP, who had connections with The Dderw, a mansion near Llyswen but within the ecclesiastical parish of Glasbury. Mrs Allen of Aberllynfi put them to shame: she subscribed £50! The school was closed in 2012, perhaps with too little consideration of the effects of its closure on the local community, and the buildings, together with an appreciable area of formerly common land, were subsequently sold with the agreement of the church authorities in what, to some people, appeared to be little more than legal theft.[7]

Wood kept a close watch in Parliament on road and tramway matters and invested in both. In 1816 the Hay Railway was opened. This was a horse-drawn tramway that linked the head of the Brecknock and Monmouthshire Canal in Brecon with the head of navigation on the River Wye at Hay-on-Wye (Fig. 4.5).[8] The tram-road was later extended to Kington.

For many miles the tramway ran through the Gwernyfed estate and its construction, with many cuttings and embankments, as at Pontithel and near the boundary of Gwernyfed's old deer park, was of much interest to Wood. As far as he was concerned, the tramway made it possible to transport coal to the Llynfi-Wye valley area at less cost than formerly, and also reduced the cost of lime needed for agriculture. It also reduced the cost of transporting agricultural products to the growing markets of the rapidly industrialising iron and coal regions of south-east Wales.

*Fig. 4.5 Horse-drawn trams arriving at Hay from the Brecon direction on the Hay Railway. (From a pencil and watercolour painting by an unknown artist, reference BRCNM 507, by permission of the Brecknock Museum and Art Gallery)*

Wood does not seem to have spent much time at Gwernyfed, and when he stayed on his estate he seems to have used The Lodge, in Gwernyfed Park, rather than the old mansion of Gwernyfed. The Lodge was later demolished and replaced by the Jacobean-style mansion of Gwernyfed Park. When he was in Brecon on county or other business he stayed with the Marquess of Camden, to whom (as shown above) he was related. Camden's prestigious seat, The Priory, must have proved ideal for that purpose. The Priory is located in the present Cathedral Close, within easy walking distance of the centre of Brecon and of its Guildhall.

In 1820-21 Wood sat on Select Committees of Parliament on issues affecting the poor. He also steered the 1821 Breconshire Bridges Act through the Commons and attempted, unsuccessfully, to extend the tax exemption for husbandry horses to ponies used in the south Wales iron industry. He was described as having 'a great love for speechifying'. To his credit, and at short notice, in 1821 he made arrangements to receive George IV in Brecon, where the king broke his journey home from Ireland following the death of his queen, Caroline of Brunswick.

Wood believed that flogging should remain one of the penalties in military life, although in 1824 he opposed the introduction of treadmills in prisons on economic grounds. He drew attention to Radnorshire where the gaol only had two cells and one prisoner, and Breconshire where the cost of installing a treadmill would be the equivalent 'of four county rates'. Wood also supported the established church, opposed slavery, and expressed strong views on vagrancy, Ireland and the need to repeal the iniquitous window tax.

In addition to his Parliamentary activity, Wood paid attention to his social and cultural duties. In 1825, for example, having travelled to Brecon to attend the assizes, he extended his stay to steward the October race meeting. In the following year, at the Brecon eisteddfod, he tried to reassure supporters of Welsh that 'the Breconshire aristocracy were not against its cultivation'.[9] Four years later he reminded government ministers that juries in cases in Wales should be Welsh speakers, since 'most of the evidence given by the lower classes of the people on criminal trials is given in Welsh'.

Wood's wife, Lady Caroline, became a lady-in-waiting to the queen in 1831. Although she was seriously ill in 1832, she survived another 33 years. Her half-brother, Robert Stewart (1769-1822), the second Marquess of Londonderry, had been Foreign Secretary from 1812 to 1822 and had played an important role in the Congress of Vienna of 1814-5. With his various links to both the royal family and to government, Wood was a man of some import. King William IV even nominated Wood as one of his executors.

His approach to the Reform Bill of 1831 was not looked upon favourably by many in Brecon, and he and his family met considerable opposition when they arrived in the town on 8 October 1831. It might even have been he who paid for the bells to be rung there that evening to welcome him!

As for the Gwernyfed estate, Wood extended it by purchasing two farms near Velindre – Cefn y Waun in 1835 and Tre-newydd in 1840 – while papers in the Gwernyfed collection dating to 1840-43 relate to purchase of the Pipton estate from Thomas Morgan. Apart from gradually extending the Gwernyfed estate, Wood's main interests outside Parliament seem to have centred on Littleton and Middlesex, where he was Colonel of the East Middlesex Militia.

His younger brother, David Wood (1812-1894), was a professional military man. He served in the Royal Artillery against the Boers in the Cape of Good Hope (1842-1843), in the Crimea (where he commanded the artillery at the Battles of Balaclava and Inkerman), and in India (to suppress the Mutiny). He commanded the field and horse artillery at the final siege of Lucknow and in 1877 he attained the rank of General.[10] He died at his home in Sunningdale, Berkshire, in 1894 and features in Elyned Wood's memories of her Victorian childhood (Chapter 5).

When Thomas II died in 1860 he was succeeded by his son, Thomas III. Thomas III was educated at Harrow before embarking on a military career and commanding the 3rd Battalion Grenadier Guards during the Crimean War (1853-56). He ended his military career with the rank of Lieutenant-General. Like his father, he was interested in politics and was MP for Middlesex from 1837 until 1847.

The year after Thomas III left Parliament, and at the somewhat advanced age of 44, he married Frances Smyth (1820-1892). She was the daughter of John Henry Smyth (1788-1822) and Lady Elizabeth Anne Fitzroy (1790-1867). Lady Elizabeth was descended from King Charles II and one of his mistresses, Barbara Villiers (1640-1709), Countess of Castlemaine and subsequently the 1st Duchess of Cleveland. Another of Barbara Villiers' descendants was Augustus FitzRoy (1735-1811), the 3rd Duke of Grafton and Prime Minister in the Whig government of 1768-1770. The Woods emphasised their social and political status with the Wood-Smyth marriage. Thomas III and Frances had seven children. Their first son, Thomas IV, was born in 1853. He had been preceded by two sisters in 1850 and 1851 and was followed by further siblings in 1854, 1857, 1859 and 1862.

On the death of his father in 1860, Thomas III inherited the Gwernyfed estate and in 1862 donated a site in Velindre village, uphill of and almost opposite the Three Horseshoes Inn, as a site for a Welsh Presbyterian chapel (Fig. 4.6). *The Hereford Times* of 8 November that year reported that on the day the chapel was opened there were three services in English and one in Welsh, 'as a considerable number of the Welsh friends were present from Bronllys, Talgarth and other places'. What the donor's father might have thought of so many Welsh speakers congregating in Velindre, 42 years after he had predicted that the end of the language was nigh, is unimaginable!

*Fig. 4.6 The Welsh Presbyterian chapel, now converted into a dwelling, in Velindre. (Photo by Colin Lewis)*

In 1859 an Act of Parliament had been passed to enable the Hereford, Hay and Brecon Railway to be built. Unlike the Hay Railway which opened in 1816 and was horse-drawn, the proposed new railway would be steam operated. The contractor was Thomas Savin (1826-1889), who built many lines in Wales and the Marches. He had previously formed a partnership with David Davies (1818-1890) of Llandinam, the great railway contractor, colliery owner and industrialist. They became the main contractor for Cambrian Railways.

Savin invested in some of the railways he built, but was bankrupted in 1866, shortly after the opening of the Hereford, Hay-on-Wye & Brecon Railway. This had occurred, to great rejoicing, on 26 September 1864 and the railway rapidly had a major impact on the Gwernyfed estate and other areas.

Prior to the advent of the steam-driven railway most local needs were catered for by local craftsmen. Iron goods were made by local blacksmiths, clothes were made by local tailors and seamstresses, flour was produced in local water mills, flannel and other woollen goods were spun in local mills, (reflected by the name 'Pandy', the Welsh for a woollen mill), even boots and shoes were made by local craftsmen, and carts and wheels by local carpenters and wheelwrights.

Suddenly, with the cheapness and ease of transport brought about by steam-driven trains, it became less expensive to import mass-produced goods rather than to make them locally, and this had a resulting effect on the economy and society. Additionally, people were able to travel far more easily than in pre-railway days, and in relative comfort even over long distances. As the *Hereford Times* of 1 October 1864 reported:

Instead of going to the coach office in Broad Street, and paying down a considerable sum even for a seat on the outside, we have only to go to the Barton Railway Station, pay a trifling sum at the little window, receive the ticket courteously rendered, take our seat in the convenient carriages, and on a twinkling we are shaking hands with our friends in Hay.

The days of coaches and horses, coachmen and guards, ostlers and rubbers, even of coach-makers and painters, harness makers, coaching inns and all the other occupations and buildings associated with the coaching trade, drew to an end with remarkable rapidity once railways opened. The Three Cocks Hotel, for example, ceased to be a coaching inn and the excitement of watching fit fine horses and liveried coaches dashing up to the entrance, grooms rapidly unharnessing sweating horses and speedily replacing them with new teams raring to go, while travellers hurriedly fed themselves and quenched their thirst, soon came to an end.

Horses were now used mainly to convey people short distances to and from railway stations, rather than from distant town to distant town. They were also used to move goods to and from railway stations, rather than to and from tram roads, river and canal barges. The days of pack horse transport, or even of long distance horse-drawn transport, rapidly ended.

In or adjacent to the Gwernyfed estate a number of railway stations were built, including Three Cocks Railway Junction which linked trains to and from mid- and south Wales with those to and from London and the Midlands (Fig. 4.7). Railways engendered new societies, and railwaymen became a new group in local life. This is reflected in J.W. Hobbs'

*Fig. 4.7 Three Cocks Junction c.1900. The Hereford and Hay-on-Wye line is on the right of the signal box. This line was commonly referred to as the 'butter and eggs line', since many passengers brought those commodities to market on trains on this line. (Photo courtesy of Glasbury History Group)*

contribution to this book which forms Chapter 7. The line to Hereford was taken over in 1876 by the Midland Railway and, following Nationalisation after the Second World War, was closed in 1962 for passengers and completely in 1964.

The last-born child of Thomas III and Frances was Charles John Wood (1862-1902). He married Mary Ashton Oxenden, daughter of Ashton Oxenden (1808-1892) and Sarah Bradshaw, daughter of a London banker. Ashton Oxenden was Bishop of Montreal before returning to England. He was a prolific writer and his *The pathway of safety*, published in 1856, was 'much appreciated by the poorer classes': it sold 350,000 copies.[11] Oxenden, with his interest in 'the poorer classes', may well have influenced his daughter's brother-in-law, Thomas IV when he became proprietor of the Gwernyfed estate after his father's death in 1872.

In 1872 the estate covered just over 5,000 acres and produced an estimated annual rental of £4,918. In 1873 Thomas IV Wood was listed as one of the seven County Magnates of Breconshire (the others were: Sir J.R. Bailey, the Duke of Beaufort, Lord Camden, Mrs Gwynne-Holford, Lord Tredegar and Penry Williams). What could Wood do to uplift 'the poorer classes' and improve his estate?

Thomas IV Wood (1853-1933) (Fig. 4.8) was educated at Eton before joining the Grenadier Guards, with whom he saw action in the Sudan.[12] Soon after he succeeded his father in 1872, according to John Bateman's *The Great Landowners of Great Britain and Ireland* which was published in 1883, he owned 9,978 acres of land, worth a gross annual valuation (gav) (as calculated for levying rates under the Poor Law) of £12,419. Most of his land lay in Breconshire: 3,796 acres (gav of £4,088); with 1,820 acres (gav of £2,870) in the North Riding of Yorkshire; 1,428 acres (gav of £2,633) in Middlesex; 1,071 acres (gav of £1,421) in Surrey; 875 acres (gav of £538) in Carmarthenshire; 601 acres (gav of £249) in Cardiganshire; 305 acres (gav of £460) in Oxfordshire; and 82 acres (gav of £160) in Radnorshire.

On the basis of acreage owned, Wood ranked in Class V of the seven ranks that Bateman recognised as 'Great Landowners', and with just under 10,000 acres would have put him well within the 1,500 major landowners in Britain and Ireland. Even more tellingly, with an actual income of between £10,000 and £20,000 generated from his landholdings, he was one of the 860 wealthiest landowners.

In December 1874, Littleton, the Woods' seat in Middlesex, was destroyed by fire (Fig. 4.1). Captain Thomas Wood (for that was his army rank at that time) then decided to make his seat at Gwernyfed. That decision had important and

*Fig. 4.8 Colonel Thomas IV Wood (1853-1933), photographed when he was a Colonel in the Brecknockshire Rifle Volunteers. (From a photograph in St Peter's Church, Glasbury)*

beneficial consequences for the parish of Glasbury and the surrounding area. Deciding to build a new mansion, Wood commissioned William Eden Nesfield (1835-88) as the architect. Gwernyfed Park, as it was called, was built in Victorian Jacobean style on what is thought to have been the site of the former Lodge by a contractor from Bristol between 1877 and 1880 (Figs. 4.9 and 4.10).[13]

*Fig. 4.9 The mansion of Gwernyfed Park under construction, 1877-1880.*
*(Courtesy of Mr Eric Pugh, Hay-on-Wye)*

*Fig. 4.10 Gwernyfed Park from the west.*
*(Source: postcard by Cartwright, photographer, Talgarth)*

*Fig. 4.11 Velindre School, converted to a house. (Photographed in 2016 by Colin Lewis)*

At the same time that he was planning his new seat, Wood paid attention to the educational needs of the Glasbury parish area. As recounted above, his grandfather had been involved with the foundation of Glasbury National School at Coed y Bolen, near St Peter's Church in 1816, but other schools were urgently needed to serve the needs of the upland Ffynnon Gynydd and Velindre areas, which lay about 1½ hours walk away from Coed y Bolen.

In Ffynnon Gynydd a new school was opened on land donated by Wood in July 1876, a school closed by Powys County Council in 2012. A similar school was opened on the edge of Velindre village in July 1877, also on a site donated by Thomas Wood. This school, which like Ffynnon Gynydd was a voluntary primary school under church management, was closed by Powys County Council in 1993 (Fig. 4.11).

The 1880s were the time of the Land War in Ireland, where many tenants withheld rents for political reasons. Landlords were physically attacked and their homes destroyed. Many great houses were burnt and remain today as empty shells, or have been completely obliterated from the Irish landscape. Many landowners in Britain in the 1880s feared the same fate, and landownership ceased being as popular as it had been. As Bateman wrote: 'What in 1882 is the value of Irish property to those in whose veins the pure Celtic blood flows not, I leave to others to answer. I should hardly think the extirpation of landlordism in Wales could long be delayed after its extinction across St George's Channel.'

It is doubtful that Bateman's thoughts were in Wood's head on the day in 1883 when he married Rhona Cecilia Emily Tollemache (1857-1940) (Fig. 4.12). Rhona was

*Fig. 4.12 Rhona Cecilia Emily Wood (née Tollemache), by Bassano Ltd. Rhona (1857-1940) married Thomas IV Wood (1853-1933) in 1883 and was the mother of Elyned, author of Chapter 5, A Victorian childhood, in this book. (© National Portrait Gallery, London)*

*Fig. 4.13 Helmingham Hall, Suffolk, one of the homes of Elyned Wood's Tollemache grandparents.*

daughter of John Jervis Tollemache (1805-1890), who had inherited land in Suffolk (where his seat was at Helmingham Hall (Fig. 4.13), Northamptonshire, Cheshire (where he was the largest landowner, with 28,651 acres, and had built himself a fine mansion at Peckforton Castle), and Ireland. Tollemache was High Sheriff of Cheshire in 1840, MP for Cheshire South from 1841 until 1868, and MP for Cheshire West from 1868 to 1872. In 1872 he was raised to the peerage as Baron Tollemache of Helmingham Hall, Suffolk.

Gladstone considered Tollemache to be 'the greatest estate manager of his day'. According to one writer: 'He was generous to his tenants and advocated improvement of their social conditions. He believed in a self-reliant labouring class and made popular the idea of his tenants having a cottage with sufficient land to keep a few animals. His catch-phrase for this was "three acres and a cow".'[14] Tollemache's father, Vice-Admiral John Richard Delap Halliday (1772-1837), had, by Royal Licence in 1821, assumed the surname and arms of his mother's family: Tollemache (Table 2).

The vice-admiral's father, John Delap Halliday, who died in 1794, had land in Shropshire and was descended from John Halliday of Antigua, who died in 1779. John Halliday had plantations on Antigua from which money passed to his son in Shropshire. He also had a natural son on Antigua, to whom he left £50! John Delap Halliday married Lady Jane Tollemache (1750-1802)

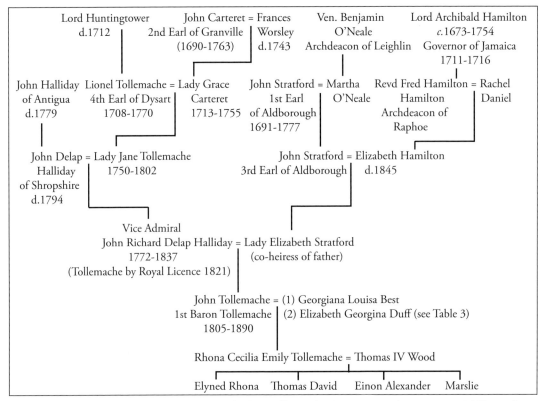

*Table 2 The four-generation pedigree of John Tollemache (1805-1890), 1st Baron Tollemache, father of Rhona Cecilia Emily Tollemache (1857-1940), the wife of Thomas IV Wood (1853-1933) and mother of Elyned Rhona Hore-Ruthven (née Wood) (1884-1965).*

in 1771. She traced back in her father's line to the Earls of Dysart and on her mother's line to the Earls of Granville.

The vice-admiral married Lady Elizabeth Stratford, the second daughter and co-heiress of the 3rd Earl of Aldborough. Through that line Lady Elizabeth descended from Baron Baltinglass and therefore had Anglo-Irish connections. They included an archdeacon of Leighlin in County Carlow, an archdeacon of Raphoe (County Donegal) and Lord Archibald Hamilton.

Rhona Tollemache's father initially married his first cousin, Georgiana Louisa Best (1809-1846). After her death he married, in 1850, Elizabeth Georgina Duff (1829-1918), better known as 'Minnie', the mother of Rhona Cecilia Emily Tollemache. Minnie was descended from the 2nd Earl of Fife, James Duff (1752-1839) and his mother's personal maid, Margaret Adam of Keith. Elizabeth's pedigree included James Dawes of Rockspring, Jamaica, by whom, through marriage, Minnie's grandfather, General Sir James Duff (1752-1839), gained control of a considerable fortune Table 3).

After their marriage in 1883 Thomas IV Wood and Rhona Tollemache (Fig. 4.12) wasted little time in starting a family: Elyned Rhona (author of Chapter 5, *A Victorian Childhood*), was born in 1884. She was followed by Thomas David in 1885, Einon Alexander in 1886 and Marslie in 1895.

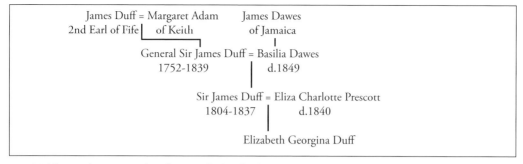

James Duff = Margaret Adam    James Dawes
2nd Earl of Fife | of Keith     of Jamaica

General Sir James Duff = Basilia Dawes
1752-1839        d.1849

Sir James Duff = Eliza Charlotte Prescott
1804-1837        d.1840

Elizabeth Georgina Duff

*Table 3 The paternal pedigree of Elizabeth Georgina Duff, 'Minnie', mother-in-law of Thomas IV Wood, and grandmother of Elyned Rhona Wood.*

Thomas IV was regarded locally as an excellent landlord, which was just as well given Bateman's prediction for the future of landlordism in Wales (see p.40), and he put much effort into upgrading farms and houses on the Gwernyfed estate. He believed in his father-in-law's concept of 'Three acres and a cow', and built a number of cottages on 3-acre holdings so that their occupiers could be effectively self-sufficient, even if they continued to work for him (Fig. 4.14).

Colonel Wood (Thomas IV had by now joined The Brecknockshire Rifle Volunteers and been given that rank) even installed water systems to serve Velindre and much of Glasbury parish below Velindre and above the River Wye. A reservoir was built above Velindre School, fed by water piped from a weir on the Velindre Brook upstream of the school.

A main pipe led towards Glasbury where there was a tank on Coed y Bolen Common, above the school. Feeder pipes supplied cottages and houses en route, including The Vicarage (now a private house, having been sold by the Church in the first decade of the present century). The Breconshire side of Glasbury village was served by pipes from a reservoir on the upper side of the railway line above Treble Hill that

*Fig. 4.14 Clarence Cottage, Velindre, one of the 'three acres and a cow' holdings, advertised as a cottage on 3 acres, 3 roods and 38 perches in the Gwernyfed Sales Catalogue of 1922. (Photo by Colin Lewis)*

terminated in the fields beside the Upper Gro where they served animal drinking troughs. An offshoot line served The Harp and other buildings beside the main road towards Hay. Another reservoir near The Kennels, above Tir-uched Farm, served pipes to Wye View, Dan-y-lan and the houses and fields from Aberllynfi House to a point nearly opposite the Baptist chapel.

Subsidiary water systems were installed from other sources, such as springs at Tyle glas, to serve the Pontithel area and fields between those points. The spring at Pontithel, which exists below the main road on the Three Cocks side of Pontithel Bridge was at too low an altitude to be piped to local houses and instead was used to serve lands and buildings down the Llynfi valley to Pipton.

Wood spent much time inspecting his estate, visiting tenant farmers and others. He was also very active in local politics and other affairs, and was a dedicated churchman, regularly worshipping with his family in St Peter's Church, Glasbury (Fig. 4.15). This church, opened in 1838, replaced an older building (Fig. 2.11) that was by then too small for the population of the parish.

The Woods were keen to improve St Peter's Church, and in 1894 the children of Mrs Frances Wood, in her memory, donated the reredos in the sanctuary that is the highlight of the building (Fig. 4.16). In 1899 Colonel and Mrs Wood had a large arch cut between the ringing chamber in the tower and the nave to admit light from the West window, which was in the tower, into the nave. In so doing the tower was weakened and subsequently cracked – perhaps they had not considered the effect on the tower of ringing the bells. The bell ringers could now be seen from the nave, and to prevent any of them from falling into the nave, Colonel and Mrs Wood donated a wrought iron screen that was installed across the lower

*Fig. 4.15 St Peter's Church, Glasbury, c.1900, where Thomas IV Wood (1853-1933) and his family regularly worshipped. Glasbury School (Coed y Bolen) is in the background to the right of the church tower. (Photo from Colin Lewis's collection)*

*Fig. 4.16 The reredos in St Peter's Church, Glasbury, donated in 1894 in memory of Mrs Frances Wood. (Photo by Logaston Press)*

part of the arch. They also had an enclosed wooden stairway installed between the ringing chamber and the choir vestry below it.

Colonel Wood employed a large staff at Gwernyfed Park, not only to serve the needs of the new mansion and its gardens, but in the stables, as gamekeepers, woodsmen and craftsmen. The Colonel was fond of sport, and ran the park around the mansion as a sporting estate, which was renowned for its shoots.

The Colonel's male employees were expected to sing in the church choir at St Peter's on Sundays and some of them rang the bells. Many pupils at Velindre School also sang in the church choir; the school's log book records for 19 September 1904:

> Several children absent all day on Monday, being members of the Glasbury Church Choir who were taken by the Vicar on their annual outing to Swansea. The teacher, Georgina Price, also obtained leave for the day to accompany the excursionists.

As described by her daughter in the next chapter, Mrs Wood's French maid made cassocks for the robed choir which sang in St Peter's and which, led by a robed crucifer, processed from the choir vestry to the chancel, and back to the vestry, at the start and end of services. The main service on Sundays was normally choral matins, with a lengthy sermon. The choir robes continued in use until disposed of by an incumbent in the 1980s.

Colonel and Mrs Wood sat in the front seat in the nave, on the south side of the main aisle. Their retainers sat behind them. The Hereford family, premier Viscounts of England with their seat at Tregoyd (about one mile north-east of Old Gwernyfed, Fig. 4.17), and their retainers, sat on the opposite side of the main aisle. Their male employees were also encouraged to ring and sing! This status-ranking continued automatically, and without any

*Fig. 4.17 Tregoyd Mansion as it was in the 1950s
when rented to the Holiday Fellowship Association. This had been the seat of Lord Hereford.
(Photograph courtesy of Velindre Village Hall committee)*

adverse comments, until the 1960s when the last of the Colonel's children, Elyned, died in 1965.

Colonel Wood was also a yachting enthusiast, to the extent that he designed one of his own yachts, and was a member of the Royal Yacht Squadron. He, perhaps extravagantly, bought Ramley House in Hampshire so as to be near the Solent and Cowes, where he sailed (Fig. 4.18).

On land, Thomas IV Wood was a pioneer of motor transport, and was one of the first car owners in Britain. He disposed of his carriage horses at Gwernyfed in 1902 and thereafter drove, bicycled, walked, or went by train.

*Fig. 4.18 Ramley House, Hampshire, bought by Colonel Wood
so as to facilitate his love of yachting.*

46

Gwernyfed Park was a home of bliss for Elyned, but as the 20th century opened all was not well for her parents. Thomas had spent too much money on improving the Gwernyfed area, on his life-style, and on building his mansion. Even before the start of the First World War he had found it expedient to dismiss many of his staff and rent out Gwernyfed Park as a sporting estate. Among those who rented it were Captain Glen Kidston (who is fondly remembered in the area[15]) and Guy Farquhar (who is remembered for the concealment of jewellery in the Park, discovered accidentally by a retriever scrabbling at a rabbit hole in 1938!), before being sold to Captain W. D'Arcy Hall. In 1910 Elyned married Charles Hore-Ruthven.

The First World War, with its terrible loss of life, including at least 15 men from the benefice of St Peter's, Glasbury, brought an end to the days of many a great estate, and Gwernyfed was no exception. In 1922 many of the farms and houses were auctioned, realising over £5,000,000 at 2016 values. Old Gwernyfed was subsequently converted into a dwelling for a gentry family, as mentioned by Thomas Perks in Chapter 6. This conversion was organised by the aged Mr Butcher, agent for the Gwernyfed estate, who lived at Penlan, near Coed y Bolen (Glasbury) school (Fig. 4.19). Gwernyfed Park was requisitioned by the army during the Second World War and was subsequently sold for educational use as a secondary school.

*Fig. 4.19 Celebrations at Velindre for the Coronation of King George VI, 1937.*
*Back row: Mr Butcher the Land Agent.*
*Middle row: Mr Davy Walter Price dressed as the king, Miss Z.A.H. Jones*
*(later Mrs Davy Walter Price) as the queen. Front row: names uncertain.*
*(Photo from Velindre School archives, courtesy of Mr Glen Smith)*

In 1937, many tenants of the estate particpated in a celebration in Velindre to mark the coronation of King George VI. The land agent, Mr Butcher, supported by the local undertaker (Mr D.W. Price as the king) and the schoolmistress (Miss Z.A.H. Jones as the queen), led a horse-drawn procession through the village (Fig. 4.19). A host of other

*Fig. 4.20 Horse-drawn procession leaving Old Gwernyfed, Coronation celebrations, Velindre 1937. (Photo from Velindre School archives, courtesy of Mr Glen Smith)*

*Fig. 4.21 Decorated hay wain, pulled by two horses ridden by liveried postilions, Coronation celebrations, Velindre, 1937. (Photo from Velindre School archives, courtesy of Mr Glen Smith)*

*Fig. 4.22 Decorated motor lorry at Coronation celebrations, Velindre, 1937.
(Photo from Velindre School archives, courtesy of Mr Glen Smith)*

people followed in further horse-drawn vehicles and there were even decorated wains complete with liveried servants (Fig. 4.21) and a decorated motor-lorry (Fig. 4.22).

After the Second World War, Mrs Hore-Ruthven, sometimes accompanied by her husband, spent the warmer parts of the year at Old Gwernyfed. She used to wander with her dogs and her memories through the grounds of what had been a great semi-feudal estate and every Sunday worshipped at St Peter's Church. In the autumn she returned to her husband's home in Norfolk. Mrs Hore-Ruthven was treated with great respect in the area, as befitted a descendant of a great Welsh family.

She often visited Glasbury Vicarage for afternoon tea. The Vicarage (Fig. 4.23) had been built under the leadership of the Revd Hugh H. Gibbon (1849-1933), vicar of Glasbury from 1883 until he retired in 1926 (Fig. 4.24). Gibbon was a graduate of St David's College, Lampeter, where he was a Hebrew Exhibitioner and a science prize-man. He became Vicar Choral at St David's Cathedral and Bishop's Vicar before being instituted as incumbent of Carew in Pembrokeshire and then of Glasbury.

At Glasbury Gibbon trained an excellent choir, was a bell ringer, and a preacher with 'an eloquent style of diction'. He was the first chaplain to Talgarth Mental Hospital and, with the support of Colonel Wood, ensured that Llanelieu church was restored and reopened. Many patients from Talgarth Mental Hospital worshipped there. One of Gibbon's successors, Vicar Lewis, had great difficulty controlling his emotions while preaching for Harvest Festival at Llanelieu in the 1950s. He suddenly realised that a whole row of female

*Fig. 4.23 Glasbury Vicarage,
where the mongoose frightened the vicar's wife
(see p.67). (Photo by Colin Lewis)*

*Fig. 4.24 Hugh Harries Gibbon by
Lafayette Ltd, 29 June 1927. Gibbon
(1849-1933) was Vicar of St Peter's,
Glasbury, 1883-1926 and a close friend of
Colonel Thomas IV Wood. (© National
Portrait Gallery, London)*

patients were wearing china chamber pots on their heads, festooned with nylon stockings! His wife, in a less prominent position in the church, immensely enjoyed the situation.

Gibbon was an active Freemason. His obituary stated that he was also 'an excellent rider and in his day kept good horses'. He had five sons and one daughter, all of whom were active members of parish life. His second son died of enteric fever while in the army in India in 1916, while his third son was wounded in action in France in the same year. Gibbon and Colonel Wood were firm friends and it may have been through Gibbon's influence that Wood edited *The Registers of Glasbury, Breconshire, 1660-1836* which was published in 1904 by The Parish Register Society, London.

Whilst Mrs Hore-Ruthven was a frequent visitor to The Vicarage, the Lewis family were also guests at Old Gwernyfed. The Revd Lewis (1910-2001) (Fig. 4.25) was a graduate in

History of the University of Wales (Swansea) and had subsequently completed theological studies at St David's College, Lampeter. He had seen service in North Africa and Italy as an army chaplain and was twice mentioned in dispatches. Lewis believed that clergy had responsibilities for the physical and educational as well as the spiritual well-being of their flocks and was largely responsible, through his influence as an elected member of the local district council and his friendship with Mrs Hore-Ruthven, for the building of Wood Villas and other council houses in Velindre. He was also influential in the establishment of the council housing estate on the edge of Gwernyfed Deer Park in Three Cocks and in the establishment of the light industrial park on and near the former site of Three Cocks Railway Junction. The Revd Lewis also played an important role in the establishment of Gwernyfed High School. He was Mayor of the Borough of Brecknock in 1976-7 and was elected an honorary alderman of that borough in 1991.

After Mrs Elyned Hore-Ruthven's death in 1965, Old Gwernyfed was rented out and then

*Fig. 4.25 The Reverend E.T.D. Lewis (1910-2001), Vicar of St Peter's, Glasbury, 1946-1984, photographed in uniform as an army padre. (Photo from Colin Lewis's collection)*

*Fig. 4.26 Old Gwernyfed in the second decade of the 21st century. (Photo by Colin Lewis)*

sold. One of Elyned's descendants continues the family connection, however, and lives on a nearby farm that was formerly part of Gwernyfed estate. Old Gwernyfed has recently been restored to some of its former glories (Fig. 4.26).

*Fig. 4.27 When Elyned Wood, author of the next Chapter, married Charles Hore-Ruthven in 1910, tenants on the Gwernyfed estate dutifully gave her a wedding present. In return they were given a portrait photograph of Elyned. This illustration is taken from the photograph given to Philip William and Ann Price of Newcourt farm, Velindre. They were tenants of the estate from 1872 until much of it, including Newcourt, was sold in 1922.*
*(Photo courtesy of Gaynor Davies, a relative of the Prices)*

# 5    A VICTORIAN CHILDHOOD *by Elyned Hore-Ruthven, written c.1960*

I was born at Gwernyfed Park, my dear home in Wales, in the early dawn of Sunday, March 16th, 1884.

A groom was sent off on horseback at a gallop to fetch the doctor. My arrival was six weeks too early, and the smart London nurse had not arrived, so the old village 'gamp' came to our assistance. She put on her best clothes to attend the lady at 'the Seat' as my home was called locally. She was dressed in a black velvet mantle, trimmed with jet beads and a black bonnet adorned with violets. My mother said she never forgot those bobbing violets!

The 'gamp' made curtseys most of the time, but she did not wash her hands, and there were no disinfectants used in those days. My mother lay in a large silver bed, with a coat-of-arms and cherubs on it.

I was told that a bonfire was lit on a hill, and rockets went off to celebrate my arrival, but it must have been a great disappointment I was not a boy.

Years after, I found a letter written by my father, at the time of my birth, to my grandmother saying, 'The little stranger has arrived, small but healthy, and is to be called Elyned Rhona.' I was baptised in our village church by the vicar, Mr Gibbon, and by my dear clergyman uncle, Willie Wood.

The first event in my life, I recollect vaguely, was my little brother's christening when I was 3½ years old. We drove to the church in a landau with two grey horses. My mother was dressed in some pale colour, and held a parasol to keep off the sun. I remember the water splashing in the font, and walking home across the park with my father. He put me on his back part of the way and I carried mother's red velvet prayer book. My fingers were hot and sticky and their impressions remained on the velvet ever after.

There was a very strict nurse called Mrs Haslam (though she was unmarried). She kept a switch in a corner of the nursery and used it freely. She bullied the nursery maid called Penelope, who wore a 'French cap' with long white starched streamers at the back.

I must have led a very quiet and ordinary nursery life. Children in those days were kept in the background, and were not allowed to be a nuisance to their elders. We were not supposed to come in the front of the house, or make a noise indoors. The nursery had the plainest of food, and woe betide me if I left a scrap of anything on my plate, however nasty!

After tea I came down to the drawing-room, hands and face washed, and dressed in a clean white starched frock, two white petticoats, a flannel petticoat, and starched drawers edged with embroidery which tickled my bare legs. My parents would read to me, or I would play a quiet game by myself.

The first thrill I can remember was to see my small brother, in a rage at breakfast, throw his lightly boiled egg full tilt against the nursery door. It made a lovely yellow splash!

I must have been four or five years old and was dressed for my walk (I wore sailor frocks, a reefer coat with gold buttons and a red sailor's cap) when Haslam took me through to my mother's rooms and said: 'I have brought Miss Elyned to show you, M'am, as she looks such a picture.' For the first time I looked in the looking-glass, and it was a bitter blow, as I was visualizing the beautiful picture by Lawrence in the drawing-room of my great grandmother in velvet and pearls.

My father was devoted to the sea and should have been a sailor instead of a soldier. When the shooting season was over and he could spare the time from his estate, he would take my mother in his yacht to various parts of the world. She was a large sailing schooner called *Livonia*, and once raced for the America's Cup.

My poor mother was terrified of the sea, and they had many hair-raising experiences in storms and fogs, and once they lost two men overboard, but her love for my father was so great she would have gone through anything for him. He was a Master Mariner and a skilled navigator.

During these yachting days, much of my young life was spent with my dear Tollemache grandparents in Cheshire, Suffolk and St James's Square, London. So many of my earliest memories are about them, as I was often with them for months at a time.

I had been told to say, if I was asked, that 'my mother was over the sea and far away'. I remember a lovely lady arriving at Pecforton in Cheshire, kissing me and saying she was my mother and had come to take me home.

'Oh, no!' said I, 'My mother is over the sea and far away.'

I wondered why her eyes filled with tears, and she told me later on she was bitterly hurt I did not recognize her.

I think my grandparents must have made a great pet of me and I have such loving memories of them both. When I was very small I slept in their bedroom, or in the dressing-room, and my granny's maid, Flick, looked after me.

My grandfather was a man of great character, and he wore a wig. Not because he needed it, but he had his head shaved for comfort. I loved to help him to dress in the mornings, and try his wig on before the glass. There was a cold shower-bath in the dressing-room, and when no one was looking it was fun to pull the string and see the water come down, but as the cistern had to be filled up again with cans by the housemaids I was forbidden to do it.

I always sat by my granny at mealtimes, whoever was there, as she liked to have me by her side. There were usually large house-parties. My mother had eleven brothers, and there were generally some of them at home. I got plenty of teasing from the uncles, and used to fly behind my granny's voluminous skirts for protection. She was very petite, with a lovely white skin and profile, and a magnificent performer on the harp; even now I can see her little hands with beautiful rings, moving so nimbly across the strings. She was very gifted and spoke Latin, Greek, Italian, German and French fluently, and had great knowledge of astronomy and literature.

They were both deeply religious and God was foremost in their daily lives.

I think they liked their home Helmingham, in Suffolk, best of all, where they always spent the summer. It was lovely to hear the church bells ringing across 'the lays' to welcome their arrival at the start of their summer stay as they drove up the avenue of old oak trees. It was a beautiful old house, with a 60-foot moat, and drawbridges which were raised at night. In the moat lived two huge pike called Jacob and Esau. Jacob always swam under the dining-room windows, and Esau's domain was by the kitchen premises.

My grandfather was very large and tall, with great personality and dignity. He always wore a black frock-coat and a top-hat even in the garden. He was a great whip, and a lover of horses, and well known in London with his four-in-hand of beautiful thoroughbred chestnuts, with long tails and manes. Horses were generally 'docked' in those days. He was friends with the omnibus drivers, who used to salute him with their whips. He had a cheery word with them and always gave way to the toiling bus horses.

He insisted on plain brown leather harness with no fitments of brass or silver, which were the fashion in those days, as he said his horses needed no adornment.

Every morning he took me to the stables to feed the horses on carrots and sugar. They were all docile except the Czar. He was a terror! The clever stable cat would jump from back to back down the lines of horses, but he always missed out the Czar.

One day when I was waiting for my grandfather in his 'curricle' outside the Houses of Parliament, the coachman said, 'Stand up, Missy. Here comes Queen Victoria.' My disappointment was great when I saw a little old lady in a black bonnet, as, of course, like all children, I expected to see a crown upon her head!

One winter my grandfather took a house in Jersey as granny's asthma was very troublesome and he thought the mild climate would do her good. They took me with them. Being very young, I only remember the rough passage, and on arrival being chased by a bantam cock which pecked at my bare legs and I ran for my life. This amused some of my uncles greatly, and they tormented me with this horrid bird. I found it hidden wherever I went. If I opened the doll's house there was the bantam cock! When I went to bed there it was again in a cage underneath. I had a little basket chair, and sure enough there was the bantam cock under it, pecking my legs! It was under the table at meals, or suddenly popped on my shoulder from behind. I was terrified, and when my grandfather arrived he said I was not to be teased any more.

Before he arrived he wrote to my Granny on her birthday, February 2nd, saying, 'I am sending you a cabbage; look inside.' When she opened the cabbage out came a lovely ruby and diamond ring. There was no registered post in those days, so it was a clever way of sending it.

One summer at Helmingham, I accompanied Granny when she presented the prizes at the village school. There were lovely prizes, and the schoolmaster's little daughter, whom I used to play with, received a very nice baby doll. I suppose towards the end I became very restive, and was banished to the schoolmaster's parlour. There I saw the baby doll on the table, reposing in its box. What evil genius made me put that lovely new white doll up the chimney? When the prize-giving was over, they came to fetch me, and little Mary wanted to show off her new doll. It was missing out of the box. Only I had been in the room.

'Where is the doll?' my granny asked me sternly. I reluctantly had to say it was up the chimney.

When it was pulled out, to my horror I saw it was pitch black. Needless to say I was severely punished, and was made to give Mary my beautiful bride doll to make up.

It was a joy when the cousins Marguerite, Winifred, Edward (Teddy) and Henry Tollemache came to stay. Edward was about my age, and a real kindred spirit. Apparently we got up to such mischief, we could not be taken out for walks together. But I only remember one incident in church when we were sharing a footstool to stand on together, as we were very small. Our favourite hymn, 'Onward, Christian Soldiers', was being sung. In our attempts to out-sing each other we began to shout and yell. We ended in a free fight, pushing each other off the footstool, and were hastily removed from the church.

The winter was usually spent in Cheshire, and we children loved to go and watch my mother and uncles skating. They were excellent performers, and did all sorts of skating tricks, while we slid about on the ice. On the way home we all stopped at a farm and had huge tumblers of thick cream. Five or six glasses full, each, went down easily.

That year, it was a bitterly cold winter, with weeks of thick snow and frost. One day Dada (my grandfather), though well over 80, insisted on driving off in his high dogcart to visit a sick tenant. He had a bad cough and, as he went off, granny said, 'Be sure and put your thick ulster on, Tollemache, as the cold is intense.'

The next thing I remember was seeing him lying very ill in bed. I was appalled, and could not understand how such a big strong man could be so ill. I did not know what I could do to please him so I made him a ring of glass beads off my doll's neck. I was touched afterwards to hear it was found under his pillow after he died.

It was a very awful time, and we children were bewildered. We were dressed up in black clothes trimmed with bands of crepe. My poor granny sat in a darkened room. My mother was broken-hearted. She was devoted to her father, and he to her as she was his only daughter. Everyone talked in whispers, and the house was hushed.

Marguerite, Winifred, Edward and I watched from a gallery the sad procession in the great hall at Pecforton, of crowds of tenants and friends who came to pay their last respects to the man who lay there. I could not believe my dear Dada was in that great terrifying box when they carried him away to Suffolk to be buried with his forebears.

A great landlord who lived for his tenants and the people around him: he was so much loved, and it was a sad day for all when they lost him.

That was the end of my happy days with my grandparents.

❧

Now I must return to my home life at Gwernyfed. As soon as I can remember, I used to ride in a basket-chair saddle on a very old pony called Brilliant, led by a very old coachman called Hogg. He had a large red nose, for which I believe there was a good reason as, the story goes, he was so drunk when he drove my Wood grandmother from Littleton, their home in Middlesex, to one of Queen Victoria's drawing-rooms at Buckingham Palace, that he galloped the horses full tilt through all the turnpikes (which were in existence in those days) without paying the fees, and finally upset her in all her feathers and jewels into the ditch.

The Hoggs lived at The Lodge, and Mrs Hogg opened the gates for the carriages. I loved her dearly. She was very old and smelt of musk. She wore a black lace cap, with a straw hat on top, and a black crochet tippet. She often gave me sweets, sugar hearts with love mottoes on them. My donkey slept in her porch and used to bray for carrots in the night.

The evening old Hogg died, a mysterious light was seen in the sky when it grew dark. It circled round and round, and finally came to stand still above his cottage. Welsh people were superstitious and said it was an omen.

❧

I am afraid I must have been a naughty child, often leading my poor little brother into scrapes. In fact, I am ashamed to own I can only remember bad things, and nothing good of myself.

One Christmas Day we were out for the first time after some illness, for a short walk in the sun with our nursery-maid Penelope. My evil genius made me take my little brother and run away and hide. Penelope called us in vain. We were soon out of sight and paddling in the brook. We both fell down in the cold water, so we took off all our clothes and laid them out to dry.

We were found eventually, in a state of nature, sitting shivering on a rock. Carried home in rugs we were put into a hot bath, and I shall never forget the sound spanking I got from old Haslam. No turkey or Christmas cake for me, and I was put to bed in disgrace.

It must have been soon after this my mother said, 'Elee, you are so naughty Haslam cannot manage you, so you are going to have a governess.' I was filled with apprehension as to what a governess might be. However, she was a very nice girl called Edith Willcocks, who lived in Three Cocks village and came up daily. She had two long plaits with brown bows. I did not learn much and she did everything I told her.

Life must have been serene and happy with the feeling of absolute security. My parents and home were my world, one could not possibly imagine it would ever change.

I enjoyed going for walks with father, generally up to Old Gwernyfed, the Home Farm, as he was a keen farmer and bred pedigree sheep and cattle. His legs were very long and mine were very short, so I trotted all the time.

I seldom left home except very occasionally to visit a beloved old great-uncle, General Sir David Wood, at Sunningdale. He had been through the Crimea and the Indian Mutiny. He called me 'the Treasure' which pleased me greatly. He had a French chef called Jules who made delicious sweets and éclairs.

❧

Every summer we went to the sea, generally the Isle of Wight as father liked to have his yacht near Cowes. The excitement of the packing and the journey was great. I liked to travel Third Class with the servants, which was far more fun than in a stuffy First Class carriage with my parents.

In those days father now had a much smaller yacht, about 40 tons I think, which he designed himself. She was a lovely yawl of varnished teak, with a graceful 'pram' bow. The seats in the saloon were covered with a bright blue material, with a design of waves and fish, which father brought back from Japan. He called her the *Maga* which is the Latin for witch, as he said she bewitched him, and he was never so happy as on the sea.

Nearly every day we went yachting, so at an early age I was taught to steer by the wind, and bring the yacht into port, and of course could row and swim and dive. One day, I made a clumsy dive and, to my horror, found myself under the keel of the yacht and could not rise to the surface. I knew she drew about nine feet of water, and thought of everyone sitting so happily in the yacht above me, little knowing I was drowning alone at the bottom of the sea. At last I rose to the surface, but not before they had put a dinghy out for me, but I don't remember being picked up.

Father also had a small racing boat called the *Morwena*. She was my mother's horror as the waves poured over her when she heeled, but father adored racing in her.

Always a bad sailor, I never really enjoyed yachting. In fact, I envied the cows and sheep grazing so peacefully on dry land as we went out to sea. I liked to wear a sailor's jersey and cap with *Maga R.Y.S.* on the rim, but I fear I was but a landlubber at heart!

❧

On return to Gwernyfed, the annual flower-show and fête took place in the park which father ran for the villages around. There was also a treat and races for the schoolchildren. I always won the hopping race and, very reluctantly, was made to give up my prize, a nice box of chocolates, to the next child. We had a band and there were speeches, followed by dancing in the marquee till dark. Altogether a red-letter day to look forward to every year.

One day, just before the flower show, I walked to the village with old Haslam the nurse, who wished to have a gossip with her friend Mrs Harris at the Mill. I was told to stay outside in the garden.

It was very boring waiting about by myself with nothing to do. I had a little stick and began swishing it about, and by mistake swished off the head of an enormous sunflower, the only one in the garden. Oh, Horrors! I knew I would be punished. So with trembling little fingers I managed to fix on the head with a safety pin and a bit of string. On departure, Mrs Harris said, 'Look at my fine sunflower, Missy. I am going to show it tomorrow at the fête!' But, alas, Mrs Harris's sunflower never appeared at the flower show.

Another treat in the summer was the visit of our dear Uncle Billy and Aunt Car, my father's brother and sister. He was then the vicar of South Mimms (Hertfordshire), and later of Mildenhall (Suffolk). He always spent his well-deserved holiday at Gwernyfed. He had a wonderful laugh and so had Aunt Car. They arrived beaming with happiness and human kindness, and laden with presents for us all.

They spent most of their time with us children, going on picnics, playing games and generally having fun. Nothing was too much trouble for them to do for others. Many visitors and relations came to stay, but none I loved so much as Uncle Billy and Aunt Car. In fact, I detested some of the old relations who came on their yearly visitations.

We were also fond of a very quaint old-maid cousin who often visited us. Her name was Laura Maria. We teased her unmercifully. She was terrified of men, dogs and spiders. She would never be alone in a room with a man, not even her own relation. She had a cock canary, but she always covered him up when she had her bath as 'he was a little gentleman'. Dogs seemed to sense her fear of them, and the least docile would growl at her approach.

Shooting parties in the winter were a great event. Large house-parties arrived in the waggonette and landau from the station, with masses of luggage, maids, valets, guns, dogs and loaders.

I was very shy and kept out of way as much as possible, but enjoyed looking over the bannisters, watching all the smart folk going in to dinner arm-in-arm, all laughing and talking, the ladies in lovely gowns and beautiful jewels and wearing sprays of flowers with maidenhair fern, made by the head gardener. The men also wore buttonholes, and had very high shiny white collars. I always thought my mother the loveliest of the ladies, and my father the tallest and nicest of the men.

A Welsh harpist sometimes played soft music during dinner, or the village band or hand-bell players played outside in the corridor.

I was supposed to be in bed, but managed to dodge old Haslam and sat in a little red dressing-gown at the bottom of the back-stairs, waiting to receive tit-bits coming out of the dining-room (especially the ice pudding) which an enormously fat and most obliging footman called Alfred used to keep for me. Though Alfred was so large and tall, he was very timid, afraid of mice, and cried when he was scolded. He fainted away when the doctor came to vaccinate us all.

Strange to say, Alfred was the cause of my tonsils never being removed. He said to me one day, 'I would not be in your shoes, Miss, as I heard the Colonel [my father] saying last night at dinner the doctor is coming to cut your throat tomorrow.' Having heard a pig having its throat cut a few days previously, I nearly died of fright and was determined to avoid this awful operation.

So the next morning I hid myself in a certain hollow oak tree, within view of the drive, where I could see and not be seen. With a quaking heart, I saw the doctor coming up the drive in his gig. It was a long time before he drove down again looking rather glum. Alfred told me they were searching for me everywhere.

I then returned innocently to the house and though I noticed a certain coldness, nothing was said as I had not been told the doctor was coming. In those days tonsils were nipped out without an anaesthetic. After that, I never dared complain of my throat if I could help it.

My donkey, Skewbald, was my great companion. I rode him every day, except Sundays, or he went for walks with us. He would follow me anywhere, even up the backstairs into the nursery, much to old Haslam's disgust. I loved him dearly and looked after him like a baby, washing his teeth with an old toothbrush every day.

He was very handsome. Pale grey with a large black cross on his forehead. He was as fat as butter as I fed him on corn. I used to sing to him, and he would bray back to me! To this day, I love donkeys more than any other animal.

What with canaries, rabbits, white mice, guineapigs and hedgehogs, my life was very full.

One year at the seaside I found, on the rocks, a young seagull with an injured wing. He was very fierce and frightened. Someone tied up his wing and I looked after him tenderly. He soon became very tame, and liked to be cuddled on my lap. I called him Chewky, as he made a funny little noise like that.

I brought him home to Wales, and he lived on a large fountain in front of the house. He looked rather lonely there all by himself. In the summer he strutted about the garden. In the winter we broke the ice on the water for him.

One early spring morning I looked out and could hardly believe my eyes when I saw *two* seagulls on the fountain. Seagulls were never seen in those parts. They swam about together all that day, but the next morning they were gone, and I never saw my Chewky again.

After that, I devoted my attention to one of the deer in the park – an old buck who had injured his eye fighting. I bathed it every day and tied it up with my handkerchief. But he soon got well and re-joined the herd. He always knew my voice and would come when I called him.

I could not bear to see helpless animals suffer and had a horror of snares and traps. Skewbald and I used to go round the places where I knew the keeper had set the rabbit wire, and liberated the poor little half-strangled rabbits. Those which were too badly injured I had to kill with a large stick. I also let the birds out of the cruel pole traps, which are against the law nowadays. I was not popular with the keepers as they had a suspicion it was I who tampered with their traps.

Pigeons were a pest to the farmers so father gave me a half-penny for every egg I found. This was a great source of income to me.

I was not allowed sweets or chocolates as they were considered bad for the teeth, so any pennies I could earn were secretly spent at the village shop on these forbidden delicacies.

I was forbidden to climb trees, as it ruined my clothes, but how could I find pigeons' eggs otherwise!

One unlucky afternoon I slipped from the top of a fir tree, and found myself suspended in mid-air by my white cotton drawers. I squirmed and struggled, but of no avail. It was getting towards dusk, and there I was, alone in that gloomy wood. At long last I heard foot-steps approaching in response to my yells, and there was the head keeper, Mitchell.

'What are you doing up there, Miss,' he said suspiciously.

'I'm stuck. Please let me down,' I replied.

He climbed up the tree, but could not unloose me.

'It's no good, Missy. I shall have to take your drawers off.'

Oh, how shocking! And I began to cry. 'Never mind', he said. 'I'm an old married man.' And it really was quite decent as I had thick combinations underneath.

I put my hand in my pocket for my handkerchief to wipe away my tears and out came a sticky mass of broken pigeons' eggs. So bang went four-pence! And a good scolding into the bargain when I got home.

When my lessons were done I was allowed to ride everywhere alone on Skewbald. A favourite ride was past the large Talgarth asylum about three miles off, as some of the poor inmates working in the fields nearby would make low bows and shout to me 'Good Morning, Your Majesty,' which pleased me greatly, and I waved my whip and shouted 'Hooray'.

Skewbald and I visited all the farms and cottages around, and my best friends were among our homely Welsh neighbours.

The ice was broken on the jug for me to wash in the winter, and a hot water bottle was unknown to me. But I had a lovely hot tub by the day nursery fire in the evenings, and the nursery teas were very cosy, the kettle humming on the hob, the fender pushed back, and we made hot toast swimming in butter and roasted chestnuts.

The nursery meals were most unappetising and generally cold by the time they got there. Mostly tepid mutton with fat, which made me feel sick – lukewarm rice or tapioca pudding. I had a passion for cheese, which was never allowed, as it was supposed to be indigestible, so I used to steal it out of the mousetraps. There were lovely peaches and grapes in the gardens, but they never came my way as raw fruit was not considered suitable for children.

On Sundays we never missed going to church, wet or fine. A long walk across the park, as of course, the coachman and horses were never used on Sundays, the service always nearly two hours long, and I had to sit as quiet as a mouse between my parents. I often made excuses not to go; that kneeling wore out my stockings, or I had a pain, but it was no good. I always had to go just the same.

My father was truly religious. Every morning when I helped him to dress he would kneel down so humbly and ask God's blessing and guidance on his busy day. His simple faith gave him great peace and dignity, and goodness shone in his face. A great supporter of the church, he and the vicar, Mr Gibbon, were firm friends.

All our maids were expected to go to church in turns. They wore little black bonnets tied under their chins. The menservants sang in the choir. Father read the lessons and took the offertory round. The organ was pumped by a blind man, and Miss Watkins, very smart with a tiny waist, dressed in mauve silk and a large hat trimmed with lilac, played the music.

It was a great event when the choirboys wore surplices for the first time. The purple cassocks were made by my mother's French maid. Some people thought it 'Popish', but the mothers liked to see their little boys 'looking like angels'. The large church was usually full, especially in the evenings when all the young people in the villages around attended. There were no bicycles or cinemas to distract them, and church was quite an event. The nursery-maid said it was fine fun, all the boys and girls coming home in the evenings. They used to link arms and sing hymns. The boys teased the girls by winding reels of cotton round them, and there was lots of harmless fun. I longed to be there too.

I am ashamed to say I took a morbid interest in what were called 'Funeral Sundays' in Wales. The Sunday following a death in the parish, the bereaved all attended church to hear the funeral sermon. The widow in a thick black crepe veil over her face from head to foot and leaning heavily on the arm of the nearest male relative, was escorted with pomp to the front pew, followed by the rest of the family as black as crows, the ladies all veiled in crepe if they could afford it. They placed handkerchiefs with wide black borders in front of them ready for use, and smelling salts for the widow. The sympathetic vicar always chose some moving text and said kind words about the deceased. The longer the sermon the better, and by then all the poor mourners were sobbing audibly. We finished up with 'Brief life is ere our portion' or 'When the labourer's task is o'er'.

In those days, there were no motorcars, bicycles, telephones, electric light or wireless, but we did not seem to need them.

Our house was considered very up-to-date with two bathrooms, one for my parents and the other for the servants, also speaking tubes to some of the rooms, and an engine outside to make gas for the lighting in the passages and back premises. When electric light was installed it was like a miracle, turning on the knob and the room became flooded with light. By standing on my toes I could just reach the switch, and loved to turn it on and off.

Now comes a period when I was rather lonely, my brother gone to school and my parents away a good deal in the winter. (Though I loved my parents, I had a wholesome awe of them and would not dream of disobeying or contradicting them.)

Neighbours were few and far between. I only had one little girl to play with. She was older and much cleverer than I, and I thought her rather a prig. I was always glad when it was time for her to go home.

She could not ride, or swim or climb trees, so one day when she came over I took her for a walk. We sauntered down to the millpond at Three Cocks, which was large and as Harris, the miller, had been grinding it was nearly empty and had a huge mud island.

'I dare you to jump onto it,' I said to the little girl, but she shuddered at the idea. 'You are bigger and older than me, so you must be a coward. Shall I push you?' I said.

She gave one glance at my determined face, shut her eyes and jumped. To my horror, I saw her disappearing in the mud up to her waist. In my remorse I jumped in to save her, but, inadvertently, I jumped on top of her, so she sank deeper in the mud. Fortunately the railway passed close by the pond and, as it happened, a train was passing at that moment. All the passengers stared at this strange sight. Luckily, a friend, Mr Jones, a farmer, was in the train. He said, 'Indeed to goodness, if it isn't that Miss Elyned.' When he got out at the nearby station he and his son kindly hastened to our help. Boards were placed across the mud for our rescue. I was fairly intact, but my poor friend by that time was licking the mud. In fact, when she was eventually pulled out she looked like a walking mud-pie.

It was a long time before her mother allowed her to come and play with me again.

Edith Willcocks by now had been succeeded by a real governess, Miss Brace, who came daily from Brecon. She was a really good teacher and I had to work hard. Breakfast was at 8 o'clock, then my round on Skewbald, before meeting her at Three Cocks station at 11 o'clock. How hard I used to pray, as I rode along, that she would miss that train. I even got off my donkey and knelt down on the wet grass. But my prayer was never granted, and during all the years she came she never once missed that train.

All the same, I was a great believer in prayer. Once I lost something of value belonging to my mother. She was away and returning the next day. Oh, how I prayed that I should find it in time. That night I dreamt it was hidden in a certain place, which I very seldom frequented. I rushed there early next morning, and lo and behold, there it was!

When children are taught their prayers, the meaning of the words should be explained to them. For instance, when I was very young, the words 'Pity my simplicity' came into my prayer. I could not think why one should pity mice and wondered who 'plicity' could be.

When bicycling came into fashion, all the world went on wheels. My parents, Uncle Billy and Aunt Car were all bitten with the craze. They went on bicycling tours in Normandy and Brittany and various parts, carrying their luggage in canvas bags on their bicycles. Ladies began to wear 'bloomers' under their skirts instead of petticoats, and elastic straps under the instep to keep their dresses down, as it was not considered modest to show their legs.

Of course, I longed for a bicycle too, but was told I was too young and they were very expensive, about £30. However, I found an advertisement in the wastepaper basket, recommending the 'Townshend' tricycle for children, price £3 10s. I was determined to have it, and set to work to save up enough money. My allowance was three pence a week, and I had won a children's competition in *The Lady* for the best essay on 'The Bravest Deed I Knew'. I could only manage to raise 30 shillings. However, father kindly made up the rest.

I shall never forget the intoxicating joy and excitement when at last the Townshend tricycle arrived in a crate!

One day I was told to come down to luncheon in the dining-room, to look after my Uncle Harry Bunbury, as he was alone. He came in late and said 'Run along and begin while I wash my hands.'

There was a wild duck to be carved. I had no idea how to set about it. With the first dig of the knife the wild duck flew over the sideboard. I grovelled for it on all fours and replaced it on the dish. The second attempt was even worse, as this time it jumped into my lap, and there my uncle found me, sitting on the floor with the wild duck in my pinafore (which children wore then) and my face all covered with gravy. He teased me about it for many years, and I still think a wild duck a difficult bird to carve.

❧

When I was about 11 years old I had a wonderful surprise. A letter arrived from my father who was in London, saying a little sister had just arrived. It was the greatest joy I could have had.

Later on in life I saw a letter I wrote to my father at the time:

> My dear father,
>       I am most pleased to have a little sister. I shall teach her to ride
>    and to swim and to dance.
>    Your affectshonate daughter,
>    Elyned Rhona Wood.

I was taken up to London to see the baby and attend the christening. She was called Marslie Joyce.

I thought Paddington station terribly grimy and noisy after the Welsh countryside. There was a yellow fog in November. The four-wheeler which took us from the station smelt of stale beer and frowst. The poor bony horse ambled along. 'My Skewbald can go faster than this,' I said, and longed to be home again.

I was delighted with the baby and loved to play with her in her nursery. Old Haslam had departed and there was a nice friendly nurse. I was promoted to a bedroom of my own and a schoolroom adjoining.

Then began a series of resident governesses, one after another, various ages and nationalities. They never stayed long. Probably they were lonely in the country with no one to associate with, and they were never invited into the front of the house. Later on they lodged in the head gardener's house, and came up daily, for which I was devoutly thankful.

❧

When mother was visiting in Suffolk, she saw a brown donkey trotting along like a pony in a butcher's cart. She had never seen a donkey trot so fast. The butcher agreed to sell it for £9, a large price for a donkey in those days, but it was a champion trotter.

The donkey arrived at Three Cocks station in a huge horse box. The porters expected to see at least a pair of fine horses to step out, but out came only one small donkey! She was called Jenny Lind after the famous singer who came from Suffolk.

Mother bought a smart little governess cart, to drive about in, but could she make that donkey trot! Oh, no! She couldn't! Nor could anyone else. So she sold it for £3 to a neighbour, and to her disgust saw Jenny trotting like the wind again.

The trap remained, so I trained Skewbald to pull it. He had never been in shafts and always tried to get on the verge where he was accustomed to be ridden. One day when the governess and I were out driving, he took fright, bolted, and upset the trap over a heap of stones. I was thrown out and cut about the face. Skewbald was struggling with his legs in the air. In my anxiety to unloose him I did not notice the governess had disappeared.

By and by, the Miss Watkins came past in their waggonette, and their coachman came to my rescue. On lifting up the trap, there was the governess, either dead or unconscious, underneath. Poor thing! She had concussion, and I had a month's holiday.

One governess, Miss McCall from Ireland, really ill-treated me, rapping my poor cold knuckles in the morning with a ruler. I hated her, and luckily discovered she was terrified of dogs. So surreptitiously I used to set my Welsh collie Rose at her. Dear Rose would pull at her skirts and pretend to growl at her. To my great joy she soon gave warning and departed.

Only one governess I was really fond of, a German called Fräulein Hubbe. Though middle-aged and rather forbidding in appearance, she was most loveable. Mother often said, 'Are you sure, darling, that Fräulein is kind to you,' and seemed surprised when I always answered in the affirmative.

She taught me to play croquet. Only the grown-ups played lawn tennis, with odd crooked shaped racquets. In the evenings Fräulein and I played halma, and I became very keen on the game.

Talking of halma reminds me how once again one of my prayers were answered. To my horror one day, mother told me, 'You are to go out to tea by yourself tomorrow with the old Miss Notts. They are very fond of you and it is rude to refuse.' I was desperately shy, and terrified of these old ladies, also I had never been out to tea alone before. I prayed fervently to be spared this ordeal, but if I was obliged to go might I play halma.

The next day off I had to go in the dogcart, in fear and trembling. Imagine my delighted surprise when, after tea, one of the old ladies said, 'And now, dear, would you like to play halma?' After that I often rode over to play halma with them.

I now had a pony called Robin but I always loved my Skewbald best. I rode most days with the coachman on one of the carriage horses riding behind me. Robin was not a very good pony and was also used by the keepers for the game cart. Sometimes I went out with the Brecon Harriers if I could get off my lessons. Of course, one rode side saddle. It would be a scandal to see a girl astride.

In Victorian times the village people were very poor, often coming up to our house for various necessities. There was always plenty of really good soup going for those who wanted it, also flannel petticoats and warm shawls. One old woman, called Everina Saunders, was constantly coming up for petticoats, so one day I nipped up her skirts and found she already had four petticoats underneath! She could not read or write, but made most beautiful smocks for her husband, working hunting scenes, flowers and animals in the smocking.

Another village character was 'Tommy the Double Digger'. He dressed in rags and was slightly 'touched', but quite harmless. He would shout and yell and wave his stick, so some folk were afraid of him. But he and I were good friends. He often walked alongside me when I was riding, talking half Welsh nonsense. Sometime he got round me to give him some coppers for a drink. This I always regretted as he was very wild after when he came out of the inn. He slept in a disused oven in some old brickworks. When a farmer killed a sheep, he would beg for a bit of the flesh and eat it up raw with his hands.

Another character was John Meredith. He was very old and a little queer. I teased him so much, which made him worse. He would chase me with a chopper, but I was too quick for him. And when I used to hide his dinner he could have murdered me.

My special chum was Mary Williams, always called 'Mary Dick'. A widow and incredibly old, she was a small ancient figure bent double with hard work: a witch-like face the colour of a walnut. Her huge hooked nose nearly met her chin as she had no teeth. She had piercing hawk-like eyes, wore very old clothes and hob-nailed farm boots. She worked in the fields in all weathers like a man, with a piece of sacking over her shoulders. She smoked a pipe and lived in a tiny thatched cottage. I often went to see her and took her dainties which I had stolen from the larder, much to the cook's disgust, especially when I once took Mary Dick a lovely trifle which had been made for the dining-room lunch. After that, the larder door was locked and I had to get in by the window.

Mary Dick and I were really great friends and she always tried to imitate me in various ways. She went to church because I did, and sat in a pew next to me, staring at me all the time so that she could copy all I did. She could not read or write, but when I turned over a page in my prayer book, she did the same. When I picked up a hymn book, she did likewise. I am afraid I sometimes took up my hymn book at the wrong moment, on purpose to see her do so also!

She always addressed my father as 'Your Honour, Squire Sir,' bobbing curtseys as she spoke.

When the time came for me to be confirmed she wished to be confirmed also. So we walked up the aisle together to the bishop. She wore a piece of white curtain on her head as a confirmation veil. Coming down she clattered out of church as fast as she could in her hob-nailed boot, thinking the service was over. She lived to a great age and was hale and hearty to the end.

The years pass by. I got into the 'teens, and begun to put away childish things. Life went on uneventfully, and I little realized that before very long I should have an unexpected shock which would quite change my present way of life.

In the meantime, once a week I attended a dancing class in Brecon where I met a few children of my own age. The governess took me by train. It was a good day's outing, lunch in a shop, and no lessons.

I learnt to play the mandolin and performed at local village concerts accompanied on the piano by the governess. She was a rather vague Frenchwoman, and on one occasion she played the wrong tune, so the mandolin tinkled an Italian melody, while the piano drummed the British Grenadiers. To my relief, everyone kindly clapped and we were asked to play an encore!

By this time most of childhood's pets had died off, except my Skewbald, who was enjoying a happy retirement, and Rose the collie. I now had a mongoose called Ricky. He was most affectionate and intelligent. He followed me about everywhere, was trained to the house and slept on my bed. When he was angry he would bristle up like a hedgehog and make wild metallic growls. The dogs had a great respect for him and always moved off the hearthrug at his approach. In the winter he disappeared, returning again in the spring in a woebegone condition. Needless to say, the French governess loathed him, and called him 'une bête feroce'.

He had a tiresome habit of going off by himself to the Vicarage, about a mile away. Why, I cannot imagine, as he was far from welcome. In fact, the vicar's wife was terrified of him, as she knew he was liable to spring at strangers if they touched him. Late one dark evening, a boy arrived breathless to say would I come at once as the mongoose had got into the vicar's wife's bed, and they dared not touch him. So off I had to go with a lantern and bring the truant home. I am sorry to say he was also unpopular with dear Uncle Billy who put bicycling clips on his trousers to prevent Ricky running up his legs. However, Ricky was most useful in the house, killing all the flies, wasps, rats and mice. He was a faithful friend, and I loved him dearly.

※

As I grew older I was more often with mother and father, and went about a good deal with the latter, walking or on ponies when we went to farms under the Black Mountains. He lived for the people around him, helping them with their family and money affairs. Everyone seemed to come to him with their troubles, and said he was their best friend. All the same, it was not always easy for him, and often a great deal of tact and diplomacy was needed.

He had a busy life, up early in the mornings, with a cold bath all the year round. At his desk all the morning, interviewing the agent, farmers and various business people. After lunch, if he did not have to attend meetings or the Bench, he would go out with his gun to 'get something for the pot'. For duck and snipe shooting he had an artificial horse made of wicker and covered with a horse's skin. He and the keeper would get inside with their guns and stalk the wily wild fowl. He was very keen on pigeon shooting of an evening in the woods, and interested in forestry, pruning most of the trees himself.

After dinner he often had to bicycle off in the dark, or go in the dogcart to various meetings. Being a very good speaker, he was much in request, and often away for nights at a time. Mother used to say he was 'a willing horse, at everyone's beck and call'. They were an ideal couple, absolutely devoted to each other, and I am glad they lived to have their golden wedding.

Mother was a delightful companion, full of charm and fun. Father, on the other hand, though he had a great sense of humour, was rather serious minded. However there were several tales of his daring adventures when he was a young Guardsman in bygone days. He once won a bet of £100 that he would drive his coach unchallenged round the courtyard at Buckingham Palace. I was told he arrived driving his four-in-hand at the Royal Military College, Sandhurst, when he joined as a young cadet. But this may not have been very unusual, as there were few trains in those days, and his home was about 50 miles off.

Now that I was older, I began to enjoy the shooting parties, and really felt I was growing up when I was allowed down 'to dessert' at dinner, dressed in my white confirmation dress. I had no party frock as there were seldom any children's parties in the neighbourhood.

Father taught me to load for him out shooting and I made myself useful picking up the birds and looking after the dog. I was very proud of father as I always thought he shot better than most of the other guns. I was thrilled one day when someone said to me, 'Your father is among the best shots in England'.

In those days beaters were paid 2s 6d a day with lunch and beer, and the boys (used as stops) a shilling. The latter were very inefficient and often wandered away from their posts, so father had dummies made, cut out of wood, instead. They had painted faces and bright coloured dresses and loose arms which waved flags and bells in the wind. They were stuck in the ground where required, and removed after each beat to other places in a farm wagon. There was always a lot of chaff about the cartload of painted ladies!

The guests were always very kind to me, but I was still very shy. Partly due, I think now, to being brought up with the idea children should be seen and not heard.

I think there must have been a great number of shooting parties in those days, as I overheard my parents discussing they had been asked to over 40 parties, and did not know which to accept.

My first romance was a dismal failure, and my heart nearly cracked! At that time I was absorbed in Sir Walter Scott's novels and my head was full of sentiment and chivalry.

Every year, during August, we made an expedition on ponies to a monastery on the top of the Black Mountains founded by a monk called Father Ignatius. On a certain date he once saw a vision of the Virgin Mary appear before him near a bush. To commemorate the anniversary a procession always took place from the chapel to this memorable spot. It was a picturesque scene, the procession of monks and acolytes in their red cassocks and surplices, swinging censors and chanting, over the heather on the wild Welsh mountainside.

Before the ceremony we lunched with some friends who lived near the monastery. On this occasion they had two other guests, a young Danish baron and his mother. He was the most wonderful young man I had ever seen, very tall with golden hair and blue eyes. A regular Viking! I could hardly take my eyes off him. After lunch he asked me to go and pick bilberries with him, so off we went. I was speechless with shyness, especially when he kissed my hand and said he had quite fallen in love with me, and would never be happy till he saw me again. I heard myself weakly telling him where I lived. Very few bilberries were picked, and we were late for the service.

I rode home in a dream. This, of course, was real romance, a white satin dress and wedding bells in the near future! (Aged about 14!) Every day I gazed at the far mountain path from my schoolroom window, waiting for the gallant figure of the gay Baron Rudolf coming for my hand in marriage. But, alas, he never appeared, and my heart sank deeper and deeper as the days passed by. My governess thought I was bilious and gave me a dose of castor oil.

Soon after this, the South African war broke out against the Boers. It was so far away it did not make much impression. Most people thought it would soon be over, but father who had fought at Tel-el-kebir in the Egyptian War in 1882, thought seriously of it. It seemed odd to me, soldiers in drab coloured uniforms to go with the veldt, instead of their bright coloured scarlet tunics.

The mandolin and I were much in request playing 'The Soldiers of the Queen' etc in local concerts in aid of the war.

Father taught me to play billiards and I rather fancied myself at the game, having once made a break of about 20!

One day he said just as he was going out, 'Oh, by-the-by, I am expecting Mr A. on business. I don't know him, but look after him till I come back.' Mr A. arrived just as I was cleaning out my rabbits. I did not know what to do with him.

'Would you like a game of billiards?' I said, anxious to show off my prowess. He said he would be delighted, and we adjourned to the billiard room. He started off first, and when father returned, quite half an hour afterwards, he was still playing, and I was standing all forlorn still holding my unused cue. He turned out to be a well-known professional player! All the same, I thought he might have given me a chance!

As I had never been bridesmaid before, it was a great event when we went to Suffolk for my Aunt Ruth's wedding. She was father's youngest sister and was to marry a distant cousin, Edward Newcombe of Feltwell Hall, near Brandon. They were both middle-aged, and he, poor man, had a wooden leg. The wedding took place from Uncle Harry Bunbury's house, Barton Hall, near Bury St Edmund's.

I enjoyed staying with my cousins, Cissy, Charlie and Bill Bunbury. Cissy was so sweet and lovely. She played and sang most beautifully to the guitar, and was very talented.

We bridesmaids wore white mousseline de soie dresses trimmed with masses of tiny white lace frills; and large white hats with wreaths of poppies, cornflowers and wheat, which were considered appropriate as Uncle Eddie went in for farming. Father gave the bride away and the happy couple started off in a four-wheeled dog-cart to drive across England to Gwernyfed, about 220 miles. They had a favourite mare called Betsy in the shafts. They arrived eventually, but it was too much for poor old Betsy and she died before they got back to Feltwell, so they had to finish the honeymoon by train.

In those days it was often the custom to travel to house-parties by train with a lady's maid and a footman in livery with a cockaded top-hat. His duty was to look after the luggage as there were constant changes, and come to the compartment with fresh hot water foot-warmers at the various stations. There was no heating or lavatories on the trains. A dim oil lamp was lit in the railway carriage when it grew dusk. The footman, on arrival, also waited on you at dinner, and helped to wash up.

There were generally seven courses. Soup, fish, entrée, joint, game, sweet and savoury, and, of course, dessert and coffee. The plates and dishes were often of silver. For a party of twenty there would be one hundred and sixty plates alone to be washed, not to mention dishes, glass and cutlery.

❧

And now comes the shock of my young life. So unexpected! So shattering!

My parents announced to me that we were leaving Gwernyfed for a year or two, and going abroad. A year or two at my age seemed to be forever. I could not believe it was true. My heart stood still. What would happen to my Skewbald, Ricky the mongoose, my collie, my pony? 'I could never leave my darling home,' I said. 'I would rather remain there all by myself.' But I was told that was impossible, as it was going to be let, and I must find homes for my pets. In fact the horses and all were going to be sold, the coachman, groom and all the servants would have to leave. It seemed to me the end of all things.

Apparently father had spent freely on the estate for many years. He put running water into every farm and cottage as he did not like to think of women having to carry heavy buckets of water. This cost him thousands of pounds, and what with doing up farms, building cottages, not to mention endless subscriptions, charities, and expenses, he felt he ought to economize for a bit. Also I was told it would be good for my education to go abroad before I grew up.

As the dreaded day of departure drew near I felt ill with misery at the thought of parting with my Skewbald, Ricky, and Rose who I never saw again. The sad goodbyes to all my village friends, the lovely Allt Wood with its bubbling brook where we used to paddle and catch trout, the Black Mountains, the River Wye, my happy home and all the dear familiar places; I left with a tear trickling down my face.

*Elyned was to be educated at a convent near Hyères in the south of France, where her parents went to stay. Although hating it at first, she grew to enjoy it. Her father took to owning cars, having been introduced to them by Charles Rolls, who drove out to visit them. The family moved to Switzerland in the summer, her father driving the car there, an event recorded in the French and Swiss papers (this was 1899). Having eventually enjoyed being away, Elyned was then sad to return to the UK, just as the Victorian era came to an end.*

# 6  LIFE AT GWERNYFED IN THE 1860S

Thomas Perks wrote this account in 1937, during which time he received an unexpected letter from Mr C. Butcher, the old Land Agent for the Gwernyfed estate (Fig. 4.19). Butcher was then was aged 87 and had served the estate for 62 years. He wrote that he was busy altering and renovating Old Gwernyfed for Mrs Hore-Ruthven. This was the old mansion, then used a farmhouse, in which Perks had lived as a child and which he describes below, together with life on the farm.

## The farmhouse

The farmhouse, known as Gwernyfed Hall, was an old and spacious Elizabethan mansion. In earlier times this had been the mansion for the Gwernyfed estate, but it had been replaced by a more convenient building in Gwernyfed Park.

Gwernyfed had stone mullion windows and an old porch – reputed to have been part of a nearby church which had long since disappeared. The interior was rambling, abundantly roomy, but inconvenient, draughty and cold. There was never any question of over-crowding, and the supply of fresh air was unlimited.

Within the porch was a massive oak door studded with large nails. This door, when opened, left a space through which many present-day cars [of 1937] could be driven. In the centre of this door, and part of it, was a smaller door which was large enough for a single person to pass through, but not without stooping. For ordinary use this sufficed. The larger door was not frequently used. To open it was a big job.

The door was the principal entrance to this part of the old mansion. It led into a stone-flagged hall, the partition structures on either side of which were ancient. Originally the hall was not partitioned from what had been a very large dining hall or assembly room. Above the partitioned hall was a chamber known as 'The Minstrels' Gallery'. This was supported by pillars which were incorporated with the ancient partitions.

On one side of the hall was a large parlour, very little used as such. On the other side was a splendid dairy. As this had a window at each end – east and west – and had another part of the old mansion to the south, it was well ventilated, always cool, and admirably adapted for storing cheese, butter, eggs and cream, and for cooling the morning and evening supplies of milk.

There was an older part of the mansion in ruins and ivy clad, but my mother remembered it in better repair. There was also a room in which it was reputed that King Charles I once slept. [King Charles dined at Gwernyfed on 6 May 1645.]

There was no water laid on in the mansion. The drinking water as well as the water required for cooking and butter-making had to be carried from a well at least 100 yards away. The only method of obtaining hot water was a kettle or a large boiling pan on the kitchen fire. In the winter mornings people had to make the best of cold water, sometimes from a frozen jug!

### Our household

Our household consisted of my widowed grandmother, Jane Probert (whose maiden name was the not very distinguished one of Jones), one of her five daughters, who became a widow at 28 years of age, and her four children. The eldest of these was myself, aged seven, then a brother aged six, a sister aged about two, and a baby brother aged about eight or nine months old. My grandmother's other four daughters (there was no son) were all married, so my grandmother was left alone with my mother and us. Although we were a large addition to my grandmother's household, we were not unwelcome, there was room for us all. Although we did not experience many of the amenities of life, we were well, if plainly, fed and really quite well housed. Anyway, we grew and thrived! Three of us were still alive in 1937, the youngest being nearly 71 whilst I'm approaching 78.

Nearly everything we ate was home-made. Bread was baked in a large brick oven heated by an internal fire of wood logs. The flour was ground at the local corn mill from our home-grown wheat. All the butter and cheese was made in the house. Milking was done twice a day. The bacon and ham were home-bred, fed, and cured. Tea and sugar were bought in the market town but hardly anything else except salt, soda, soap and blue [used in washing clothes]. The only intoxicant was cider, and that was made at home, too. Very little was bought from the butcher. A sufficient supply of mutton was always available from the home flock and for some years during my earliest recollections a bullock was killed in the autumn and salted, providing a considerable supply of salt beef.

The farm and rickyard were, of course, an admirable poultry run, and in their seasons produced fowls, ducks, geese and turkeys. Chickens were not killed for home consumption.

There were generally two maids in the household, and they had enough to do as all the unmarried men who worked for my grandmother 'lived-in' and occupied quarters of their own, they were boarded as well as lodged. Besides, all the milking was done by the maids, and sometimes the butter churning too if, by stress of circumstances, a man was not available.

### The centre of household activities

The large kitchen was the centre of all household activities. It had a large open fireplace. Over, or in front of that fire nearly all the cooking was done. Meat was more often boiled than roasted. Boiling produced broth which was served to the farmhands at an early breakfast, or last evening meal.

In the fireplace was fixed a small crane apparatus called a 'sway'. This would swing out from the chimney-back across the hearth and much facilitated hanging a large pan or boiler over the fire. Any roasting that was done was usually on a turnspit in front of the fire. It was operated by a 'Jack' that was wound-up. It used to be a privilege to baste the joint or goose which was being roasted.

The kitchen was plainly furnished with a well-scrubbed oak floor which had no covering whatever. There were three interesting features. One was a large substantial black oak table long enough to seat about ten each side. This was very old. The last time I saw it was as an exhibit in the County Museum in Brecon.

Another feature was a 'long-cased' grandfather clock. This was very old, of oak, and bore the name of the maker living in the local market town. It was the only clock in the house that would go! It was always of great interest to us children old enough to be up at the appropriate time, to watch its being wound up. This occurred every evening. It was done by a chain and pulley, and presently the heavy weight bobbed-up from below.

The third feature was a large rack suspended from the ceiling, called in that locality, the 'cratch'. To this were hung flitches of bacon and hams.

Nearly a third of one wall of the kitchen was covered by a wooden dresser, as was common in that district for holding plates and dishes. When they were placed vertically in the shelves they had a decorative effect.

### Home products

Yarn spinning as a home industry was declining at this time, but most stockings were of home-grown wool spun and, of course, hand knitted. There still remained several treadle-driven spinning wheels. They were not then appreciated and were gradually broken by mischievous young folk of whom I must confess to having been one!

Welsh flannel was certainly – and I think blankets too – made of home-grown wool. But they were woven at a factory in the next county. Whether the flannel and blankets you got back were the produce of your yarn was a problem, as it also was with whether the flour the local miller sent you back was ground from the wheat you sent to him!

I don't remember anything that we slept on except feather beds. These were home-produced, there being plenty of feathers accumulating from the dressing of the denizens of the poultry yard. The beds varied in quality according to the grading of the feathers.

Candle making was an annual task my grandmother did herself. The tallow came chiefly from mutton-fat. The plant for the 'factory' was as simple as the job itself. First there was a long deep narrow box into which was poured the melted fat. Next, there were a number of rods a little longer than the box: over these were hung a number of double wicks. Then there was a frame not as wide as the rods were long, to hold the rods and wicks for cooling.

The process was to take each rod separately and dip the hanging wicks into the hot fat, then to place them across the framework to cool. When you had done this with, say, 20, the first you had dipped would have cooled enough to be done again. Of course, the first turn did not leave much tallow on the wicks, but gradually, by repeating the process, the candles took shape. When finished they naturally had a stalagmitic appearance, as the butts of them thickened more rapidly than the tops.

I only remember one oil lamp in ordinary use; the usual illuminants were these home-made tallow candles. The candles were not too effective when used, however, and required constant 'snuffing' to prevent smokiness and a dimming light. Snuffing was accomplished in various ways. The proper method was by a pair of 'snuffers' constructed after the plan of a pair of scissors, but which had a small box on one blade of the scissors into which the operation of snuffing carried the charred wick. A pair of scissors would do if the snuffers were not at hand. Failing both, wetted thumb and finger sufficed. This last method was tricky, and only to be ventured on by an expert.

I think it was in a candle-maker's brochure that I read the reason why snuffing became redundant. It was discovered that by twisting one wick more tightly then the other, it would have the effect, when the candle was burning, of making the charred part bend over. The point of the wick then gets burnt to a fine ash, which falls off. The candle thus snuffs itself.

My grandmother was a stern ruler in the matter of 'early to bed, early to rise', consequently the use of artificial light was kept to a minimum.

## The farm lands
The farm which went with the old mansion house was about 300 acres in extent. A considerable part of this farm was good arable land. The crops grown were wheat, barley, oats, clover and turnips, but not hops, peas or beans. There was, for that elevation above sea level – about 500 feet – considerable orcharding. In addition there was a 'sheep-walk', which was an area of unfenced mountain land used for grazing sheep during the more clement phases of the year. The sheep-walk was about six miles away on the dip slope of the Black Mountains.

At the time of my earliest recollections two other smaller farms were held as 'bytacks'. Bytacks were farms subsidiary to the main farm. They were mainly used for grazing sheep and, to a lesser extent, cattle, especially in the winter when sheep had to be brought down from the mountain sheep-walk. There was not much plough land on these additional farms. In more recent times farmers from our area began to send animals 'on tack' to west Wales in the autumn. The milder climates of those coastal and lower areas enabled the growth of grass even during most winters, thus providing fodder ('tack') for livestock from our climatically harsher and more upland and inland area.

The main farm, bytacks and sheep-walk, merited the estate agent's description of a useful mixed holding.

## My grandmother's undertaking
With the help of a trusted old bailiff, Thomas Price, my grandmother had successfully run the home farm, the two bytacks, and the sheep-walk, for many years. She had a herd of about 100 cattle, about three or four teams each of two carthorses, plus about five or six unbroken animals, e.g. yearling colts and foals, and about one thousand sheep.

The undertaking required a considerable number of men. Some of them were old stagers: the farm bailiff, Thomas Price; the shepherd, John Williams; a general utility man, John Davies; and a gardener and odd-job man, John Jones – all with Welsh surnames. In addition there were a cowman and two or three waggoners and under-waggoners, but they changed from time to time, being usually hired for a year at one of the May hiring fairs. I do not remember much about them. All the unmarried men 'lived-in' and occupied quarters of their own: they were boarded as well as lodged.

### The horses

My grandmother kept a good strain of horse flesh and the colts were valuable and easily disposed of. In addition there was an old pony named 'Jerry' and a smaller pony which the shepherd used in summer time. Mares were bred to local stallions or to stallions that travelled the area (see Appendix I).

### Working with horses

Working with horses requires experience, skill and patience. Ploughing, in particular, needs skilled hands. This showed well at the local ploughing matches. A steady team of horses and a good understanding between them and the ploughman was essential if the furrows were to be turned evenly (Fig. 6.1). Many of the waggoners took great pride in their teams and often supplemented the allowance of oats by means which the law somewhat unkindly called 'theft'. The thief got nothing from it except a more glossy coat on his horses. The condition of his team meant something to their man. Long after the advent of the railway, farm produce – wheat, barley and wool – was sent to Brecon, a distance of 12 miles by road. There the waggoners would meet in friendly rivalry.

One of the farm's waggons was known as the 'road waggon'. It was adapted for either road or farm purpose. For the road double tyred wheels were changed for narrow wheels.

*Fig. 6.1 Andy Elms competing with a team of Shire Horses in the All Wales Ploughing and Hedging Championships on 17 September 2016 on land adjacent to The Warren of the former Gwernyfed Estate. (Photo by Colin Lewis)*

*Fig. 6.2 A Shire Horse in full waggon harness, including two sets of bells, on display at the Radnor Show, 1956. (Photo by Colin Lewis)*

Also, double shafts were used. Thus on a road the team was of four horses, two abreast. One of the leaders carried a frame of bells (Fig. 6.2). This was in the shape of the letter 'U', but upside down and fastened to the horse's collar. On the underside of the rounded part were fixed several bells. These, of course, were rung by the horse's movement and announced the coming of the waggon. The roads were none too wide and suitable passing places not always available.

After ploughing was completed the land was harrowed. This was also done using horse-power. Since harrowing was lighter work than ploughing it could be done by young horses and was a useful way of training them to collar work. When harrowing was finished and the land was suitably dry, sowing could be undertaken, this was normally done by hand through a process known as 'broadcasting'.

### Broadcasting (sowing by hand)

My admiration was always aroused by the way the bailiff, Thomas Price, could stride down the furrow with his 'seedlip' suspended just above his waist, filled with seed wheat, and first with one hand and then with the other, scatter the grains evenly over the ridge. There was a subtle reason for this and why it should be done well – upon the evenness of the sowing depended the regularity of the ultimate crop. But beyond that, all the countryside knew who was the sower, and when the corn came up all could see how well or ill the job was done. If ill, it was an eyesore and a heartache for something like nine months and a great opportunity for rustic comments.

Thatching a rick with straw also required great skill. Hedging and ditching, particularly 'laying' or 'pleaching' a hedge, was also by no means a simple task. Like broadcasting, all three tasks, if done clumsily, were the subjects of local ridicule!

### Lack of machinery: working by hand
Farm operations were undertaken with practically no machinery, as with broadcast sowing. Reaping was done by hand with a sickle; mowing by a scythe, ploughing by a team of horses and a single-furrow plough – no tractor. Weeding and 'singling' (the thinning of crops such as turnips when the plants were young, using a three-cornered hoe) were done by hand, binding was also by hand. Threshing the grain was in a transition stage, some-times done by the portable threshing machine and steam engine that toured the district, but still sometimes on the barn floor by flail and a man's muscle-power. Sheep were sheared by hand-shears, which used a lot of energy on the part of the shearers. We did, admittedly, have a turnip cutter and a chaff cutter but they were powered by hand. The turnip cutter reduced turnips to manageable size for eating by livestock by cutting them into strips. The chaff cutter reduced hay and straw to small pieces that were more easily palatable to horses than the original material.

### Women's outdoor work
A considerable share in the outdoor work of the farm was taken by the womenfolk. In spring they weeded the corn crops by removing the thistles. They also 'set' (i.e. planted) potatoes and, later, did turnip hoeing and singling. With the coming of summer there was work to do in the hay and clover fields. In harvest time there was a variety of occupations associated with reaping and binding (see below).

Barley and oats, when cut, had to be turned to dry, and then gathered. This was done by men and women. Similarly, after harvest came potato and apple picking and later, turnip 'topping and butting'. [Pulling turnips out of the ground and cutting off their leafy tops and their roots.] These tasks, often done in inclement weather, were cold and cheerless.

A hardy veteran in field work was old Betty Jones. She was always kind to us children and welcomed us to her thatched cottage. Her husband, John Jones, did the gardening and odd-jobs. His mental attitude to boys was less kindly. To him they were 'varmints' and always getting into or just coming out of mischief. Therefore, thrashing at sight was always merited.

### Reaping and binding
It was the local custom to announce to your neighbours shearing, hay-making and 'reaping' days. They would then send one or two sons or farm-men to help gratuitously. This cour-tesy would, in due course, be returned. I have seen as many as 15 or 20 reapers, each using a sickle, in a field of some 20 acres. They were followed by 'binders' who took the bundles of cut wheat from the reapers' arms, passing a band of a few strands of wheat from the reapers and arranging the heads together and tucking the strands around the bundles. This, done

skilfully, bound each bundle of corn effectively into a neat sheaf. A boy could bind after one reaper, a woman after two.

Feeding such a company was a problem, as it was at shearing and hay-making. My grandmother solved part of it by hiring a donkey and cart from a villager and providing picnic meals on the spot. That economised time and afforded the reapers and binders a longer rest. The whole scene was idyllic. In this country the sheaves must be set-up in shocks (locally 'stocks') and left for the grain to harden.

### Threshing and winnowing

The grain was normally threshed on the barn floor with a 'flail'. This is defined in the *Concise Oxford Dictionary* as a 'Hand threshing implement, wooden staff at end of which is a short heavy stick swinging'. That is a good definition, except for the word 'stick' which suggests something like a walking stick. In fact a substantial block of wood was what it was. This is better described by the *Encyclopaedia Britannica* as a 'short thick club called a swingle or swipple and attached by a rope or leather thong to a wooden handle in such a manner as to make it swing freely'.

The method used was to cover the barn floor with a layer of the corn to be threshed, then to beat it all over with the swingle. You swung it above your head and brought it down with much force on the corn. When you had beaten the corn all over once, you turned it over and shook it up. Then you repeated the process, perhaps more than once. Eventually you cleared the threshed straw away leaving the wheat grains and chaff on the floor.

To separate the grains and chaff the primitive plan was to open wide the large doors of the barn opposite each other and hope for a good wind. By throwing the wheat and chaff up against the wind the wheat fell to the floor again, but the chaff was blown outside. The wheat was afterwards graded by passing it over a hand-shaken sieve. This method of threshing was not so thorough as that done by modern machinery, but cattle which were partly fed on straw in the winter got a little corn as well, and so did the barn-door poultry.

### Cider making

Cider making was a late autumn and early winter occupation. It required a man, a horse, a large circular trough, a heavy circular stone, a press, hair cloths and, of course, suitable apples. The greater part of the trees in the orchard were cider apple trees. The fruit was very deceptive both in appearance and taste. The appearance was very bright and tempting. The first bite was momentarily satisfactory but quickly gave way to a bitter roughness. The fruit was aptly enough locally-called 'Bitter Sweet'.

The apples were taken from the trees and gathered into heaps in the orchard. They remained there for several days to maintain a mature condition, but ultimately they were removed to a large building known as the Cider Mill. This contained a large circular trough into which the apples were placed when crushed. The crushing was effected by a large heavy circular stone similar to a millstone, but revolving vertically instead of horizontally. Through the centre of this circular stone a piece of timber was fixed – the inner end of which was inserted into an upright post. This would revolve and was itself placed in the centre space within the trough and secured to an overhead beam. The other end of the piece of timber stood out beyond the trough and to this was hitched an old horse which walked round this trough all day and day after day – until the cider-making was done.

Of course, the horse pulled the millstone which itself revolved like a wheel around the trough, and in so doing gradually crushed the apples into a horrible, nasty, slushy mess called 'mush'. This was then taken to the press and made into a 'cheese'.

The press consisted of a square table sort of structure with a channel all round except at one place in the middle of the front side of the square, where there was a hole. Around the square was a moveable frame which stood up three or four inches and could be raised higher and higher. Over this was spread a large cloth, in appearance like a blanket. Upon this horse-hair cloth was placed as much mush as the frame would hold.

The edges and corners of the cloth were then turned-in, the frame lifted to the new level, another cloth placed over it, and the whole process repeated. The result was quite a big stack of 'cheese'. As it grew bigger its weight squeezed out the apple juice from the bottom of it. The juice ran round the channel I described, out through the hole and into a receptacle placed underneath to catch it. The flow of the juice was accelerated by placing on the top of the 'cheese' a square lid with strong timbers on the upper side. The upper part of the press consisted of a stout beam which, by screwing, was forced down on the cross-timbers and so further compressed the 'cheese' until it ran dry.

That was the whole operation of cider-making. Nothing at all was added. The resultant cider was the pure juice of the apples. When it was newly made it was non-intoxicating, sweet and pleasant to drink. In colour it was much like claret.

The next stage was to carry the juicer in ordinary buckets to the cellar some distance away. It was poured into hogsheads and left to ferment. Old John Davies who did this was distinguished from other Davieses as John Davies 'The Warren', being the name of some fields near his cottage. John would have said that the cider was left to 'work'. Work it did and out of the bung holes – which for a time were left open – came a night-cap of white fresh froth and bits of apples or anything else which accidentally had got in with the cider.

Cider, like wine, changes as it matures. Tastes varied. By about March following making, the cider would be in good condition. In haymaking and harvest time it would be getting into condition which was known as 'hard'. It was then definitely intoxicating. Cider so made did not fizz like champagne. It was, in times such as I describe, always drawn from the wood and so drunk.

### *The sheep and the sheep-walk*

John Williams, the shepherd, was a loyal pal to us boys. He spoke English to us, Welsh to the dogs except when he got angry with them, and then he cursed them in English. He would tell us that there were no swear words in Welsh. He was in charge of up to one thousand sheep, although numbers varied depending on the time of year, being highest immediately after lambing and less in the autumn after the great sheep sales.

Many happy expeditions did we have with Old John in spring or summer to the sheep-walk on the Black Mountains. The distance was not more than six miles. We started from 500 feet above sea level and to get to the brow of the mountain (about five miles) we climbed about 1,700 feet. The last mile or so 'over the top' was more inclined to fall the opposite way. At the back of the mountain-top as we looked at it, and which was the ridge of that watershed, the springs began to trickle in streams flowing the opposite way. They grew larger and had, long ages ago, cut valleys for themselves.

A mile further along was our sheep-walk. This was an entirely unfenced area of mountain-top moorland. It always seemed wonderful to me that the sheep, although restless at first, when in the late spring or early summer they were taken up there after wintering at the down pastures, did after being watched and rounded up for a week or two, eventually settled down and remain on their own ground.

We never spent a night on the mountains, but Old John did, especially in the first week after the sheep's migration. His life was rather hard at that time, also in lambing time. He showed us the heap of stones around which, while joining hands, three boys could stand each in a different county. He also knew the highest point – Pen y Gader Fawr, Great Cradle Mountain in English. It is 2,624 feet above sea level. Down in a valley near our sheep-walk were the ruins of Llanthony Abbey; a situation well suited for quiet meditation and indeed 'Far from the madding crowd'. The nearby stream contained trout.

A large flock of sheep meant a lot of lambing and shearing. It was customary to tell our neighbours of shearing days so that they could come and help. We returned the compliment in due course and no money was involved on either side although everybody was suitably and generously fed.

Before the sheep were shorn they were driven into a dipping pool, which was normally a natural or dammed pool on one of the local streams. The men held each sheep down in the water with long poles, so that the sheep, while struggling in the water, washed themselves. Nobody wanted to shear dirty sheep!

Shearing was done, using hand shears, in the big barn. This had two large floors between the 'mows' in which some of the harvested grain had been stored. Each floor was spacious enough to hold a laden four-wheel waggon. Usually both floors were filled to capacity with shearers. Boys were used to catch the sheep and bring them to the shearers. These were busy days for the women, preparing and cooking meals which were served on plentiful lines. Each fleece, when shorn from a sheep, was sorted and tied into a bundle, ready to be sent with others to the market town (Brecon) for sale later in the year.

### Going to market

Almost every Thursday my grandmother went off to Hay Market in a dogcart well-laden with farm produce for sale. She drove herself and managed alone the old pony, 'Jerry'. He was very old, very safe, and very slow. The distance was five miles and the standard time was not much under the hour. She would bring home the few essentials for house-keeping, but spend as little as possible.

There was another market town in exactly the opposite direction, Talgarth. This was not visited so regularly, but more often in the summertime when poultry, butter and eggs were more available. When employment was good and trade brisk in the south Wales coalfields and ironworks, locally known collectively as the 'works', there was always a good market at Talgarth.

## The sawyers

Nearly all the farms and villages, too, in that district, belonged to a few landowners. My grandmother's farm was near the centre of the Gwernyfed estate. The estate carpenters' shop and sawpit were actually part of the very large farmyard. The sawpit was a great attraction. It was long and narrow, but a deep hole in the ground. Timber which was to be sawn into boards or scantlings was placed lengthwise over the pit. Two men worked the saw, one on the top pulling it up, the other below pulling it down. He, of course, got the sawdust. No one who has ever actually seen this in operation can fail to appreciate the advantage of being 'Top-sawyer'.

## Local conditions

For several years after the railway came to Three Cocks life for most remained relatively unchanged. The village of Velindre had two working shoemakers, a tailor, a dressmaker, a chapel, a small licensed beer-house, and two very small shops whose stocks were mainly sweets and tobacco. Of much greater importance were a smithy and a wheelwright's shop. The local people, in large measure, lived a communal life.

The village and surrounding district were a distinct part of the larger parish of Glasbury. There had not been facilities for people to wander away, so apart from visits to nearby markets and fairs for business purposes, and to get married and buried, folk stayed around the hamlet.

Of public services there were few, and of a meagre description. A walking postman came from Hay every weekday, reaching Velindre village between noon and one o'clock and departing about two or two-thirty: not a long postal day! Telegrams were delivered from Hay and the porterage was five shillings. Their use was not common.

I don't think there was a carrier or public conveyance of any kind; I certainly don't remember one. The farmers rode on horse-back, or drove a dog-cart or spring-cart. Those who were without such transport, unless they could get a friendly lift, relied on shank's pony, which was a reliable steed!

I have no recollection of any railway class except 'Third', but I have a frigid recollection of that! There was no cushioned seat, only polished wood. Sometimes, in cold weather, there were so-called 'foot-warmers'. Luckily, at that time ladies wore ample petticoats and crinolines and the best dodge for a youngster was to sit between, say, his mother and an aunt.

I have very little recollection of social entertainment. I think there cannot have been much. Nonconformity was, of course, very strong and the local chapel was an important centre for gossip and news as much as for piety. The markets and fairs were also social occasions. I cannot remember a village concert or lecture. There were no Women's Institutes or Library Centres. There may have been meetings for singing practice. The country folk were good vocal musicians and sang 'parts'. I remember at the local chapel the village carpenter sang alto, and the effort was so great that perspiration used to trickle down his cheeks.

Winter evenings and Sundays were not too cheerful. My grandmother was not well educated and not an educational enthusiast. Her native tongue was Welsh. She read English with some difficulty and spoke it inaccurately. She possessed no books except a Welsh bible, hymn books, and a few religious books. Her main idea was useful work of some sort. I don't remember playing any games at all. Cards would have appalled the old lady. Church or Chapel going was *de rigueur* on Sundays and nothing more thrilling than the 'Sunday at Home' was permissible on that day.

What I have written about Gwernyfed and the life there is, I think, fairly representative of farms of that size in that area. Not all agricultural districts of Wales were so rich and fertile. Consequently a large proportion of farms, particularly in the higher levels and on steep and hilly slopes, were much smaller than Gwernyfed. Life, in many respects, was much harder, narrower, and sterner on such farms.

# 7  THREE COCKS AND SURROUNDING AREAS, 1902-5: A RAILWAYMAN'S MEMORIES

*This chapter is a slightly altered version of Mr Hobbs' original and of extracts from his writings as published in* The Messenger *in May 1997 and January 1998, with the addition of illustrations.*

I lived at Three Cocks from August 1902 to April 1905. I was employed as a booking clerk at Three Cocks Station. It was then a comparatively busy place (Fig. 4.7). The Midland trains ran through from Swansea to Birmingham, and the Cambrian trains from Moat Lane to Brecon; during the summer trains ran through from Cardiff to Aberystwyth.

The staff at the station consisted of a station master: salary £70 per annum with free house, coal and paraffin; booking clerk at £45 per annum; two signalmen at 23 shillings each per week; two porters at 15 shillings each per week; and a lad porter at 5 shillings per week. Extra staff were supplied during the summer. The Railway Clearing House kept a number taker there. [The Railway Clearing House apportioned fares between the various railway companies when the route taken by passengers or goods used rolling stock or lines managed by more than one of the many railway companies; the number taker recorded the trains and carriages that passed through the station, which was at a junction of railway lines.][1] There were also a ganger and five plate payers at 20 shillings and 16 shillings each per week respectively.

The staff worked a 12-hour day including meal-times, except the signalmen who worked 12 hours with no meal-times allowed. The signal box was open day and night, and only closed for a few hours on Sundays.

I lodged with a fine old couple, both well over 70, and at once had a lively altercation over the terms. The old lady said her charge was 2s per week. I said I always paid 2s 6d. The old lady flatly refused to accept more than 2s, but at last we reached a compromise. I was to pay 3s 6d per week, but for this she would provide me with potatoes daily, and a full dinner on Sundays. I was not very favourably impressed with her at first, but I soon found that although her tongue was rough, she had a heart of gold, and for the next three years no mother could have looked after me better than she did.

My landlord was employed at the Pontithel Chemical Works, which was then in full swing and had a siding connection to the railway (Figs. 7.1 and 7.2). He was a great sufferer from a stomach complaint, which he attributed to the fumes from the charcoal [in the works], but which was probably an ulcer. I think of him trudging along the muddy road every Sunday to Glasbury Baptist Chapel. Rain or shine, he never missed.

The old lady had reared a family of eight, she baked her own bread, brewed her own beer, cured her own bacon and ham, and kept a pig, which provided the main food supply. A curious survival was the belief in witchcraft. She would tell me numerous stories of the happenings at the farmhouse near Bronllys where she worked as a girl. At one time my nose used to bleed every morning as soon as I prepared to wash. After a week they believed I was bewitched, and that I must go to a 'conjurer' at Bronllys who would cure me. I did not go, and they were very vexed about it, but the trouble ceased of its own accord later.

Mr Jacobs, the proprietor of the chemical works, used to conduct a Sunday School in a cottage at Pontithel. The chapels of those days were the centres of all social activities. Christian Union meetings used to be held at all the chapels in turn during the winter, and were chiefly singing and recitations. The meetings were always held at the full moon, to take advantage of moonlight for travelling. After the Welsh revival of 1904-5 some of the chapels started Christian Endeavour Societies, which did good work.

The railway company dealt with telegrams on behalf of the post office, and a large part of the lad porter's

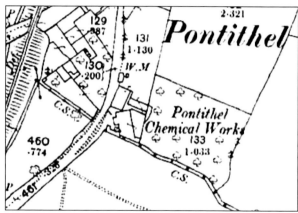

*Fig. 7.1 A map showing the location of the Pontithel Chemical Works. The section of railway line shown is part of the main Hereford to Brecon route, about 1 mile on the Brecon side of Three Cocks.*

*Fig. 7.2 The only intact building left standing at Pontithel Chemical Works in 2016.*
*(Photo by Colin Lewis)*

duties was the delivery of those. He had to deliver telegrams to Three Cocks, Pontithel and Velindre village and beyond the village right to the Black Mountains. Upper and Lower Cwmcadarn farms used to have a number of telegrams. All were delivered free up to three miles; over three miles a small extra charge was made. They were all delivered on foot, and the charge for a telegram in those days was ½d per word with a minimum of 6d. In other directions the delivery was not so wide, as those areas were covered by the post offices at Llyswen, Glasbury, Bronllys and Talgarth.

The post office was at the station, the stationmaster being also the postmaster, but the latter duty had no link salary-wise with the railway. The postmaster's salary was paid by the General Post Office (G.P.O.). The railway company granted the stationmaster permission to undertake postmaster's duties for the G.P.O. and to use the booking office as a post office. I assume the G.P.O. paid rent for the space thus occupied.

The G.P.O. employed two postmen: one was full-time at 23 shillings per week, and the other was part-time at 12 shillings per week. The part-timer was a cripple. Both postmen received uniform and boot allowances and both were employed for the morning delivery. The full-timer managed the collection in the evenings on his own.

The Refreshment Rooms at Three Cocks Station were among the best on the Cambrian Railway, and used to provide luncheon baskets on request for through travellers. Telegrams ordering these luncheons were transmitted free of charge.

One of the signalmen, Albert Delaney, was a genius. He used to make wire bird-cages, violins (out of cigar boxes), electric batteries, and his own gramophone records of the old cylindrical type. When I last heard of him, many years later, he was making wireless sets.

Delaney was an accomplished violinist, and as I was also interested in music he taught me to play. Violins could be purchased from 2s 6d upwards. After a few months we formed a band, with two violins, a viola, a flute and a clarinet. I played the viola, the number taker a violin, a porter the flute and a local farmer, Mr Lewis of Tregoyd, the clarinet. Then we wanted a bass instrument, so we purchased a second-hand cello for 10s and arranged for one of the postmen who could read music to play it.

Unfortunately, when the postman came for his first lesson we found he had lost the three middle fingers of his left hand in the Boer War, so we had to look further afield. We found a volunteer in the village blacksmith's apprentice, and in a few weeks taught him sufficient for our purpose. Later we added a male voice choir of eight singers, and we used to go around for miles singing and playing, both at private houses and the local chapels. We got quite well known. The singers included three Wilcocks from The Three Cocks Hotel, all church choir members and very good singers, and Bert Jenkins of Glasbury. Bert Mills and Albert Williams were two of the railwaymen.

All the men could read tonic sol fa at sight. This was a surprise for me as I had never seen this system before, but I soon learnt to transpose from or to staff notation. We never attempted anything great – Sankey's hymns, Caleb Simper's carols, a male voice piece called 'The sailor's choice', and Wright and Round's string band arrangements – but we thoroughly enjoyed ourselves, and were always welcome wherever we called.

Delaney, Albert Williams and myself used to play with the dance orchestra at Talgarth Asylum after it was opened, and they used to have weekly dances. The only other local

*Fig. 7.3 The Baptist Chapel near Glasbury bridge, now used as a bunk-house and canoe centre. (Photo by Dr Margaret Gill)*

players were Mr Evans, the asylum clerk, who played the cello, and Ray Willis, son of the Talgarth postmaster, who was the pianist. The leading violinist was an inmate, but I have forgotten his name.

About 1904 we had a new stationmaster who was a good singer and also a teetotaller. He had a favourite song called 'The song of the pump', so Delaney made him a model pump out of cardboard, and he used to take this to all local entertainments, with a boy to pump while he sang. He never failed to get an encore.

The churches and chapels were all well attended. There was a good choir at St Peter's, where the Revd H.H. Gibbon was vicar. There were good congregations there, chiefly the gentry, retired people, visitors at the hotel [The Three Cocks Hotel], and some of the larger farmers. Most of the working classes were chapel, except those employed at Gwernyfed or Tregoyd. The strongest chapel was the Baptist at Glasbury, which was always full on Sunday nights, and often packed (Fig. 7.3). Baptisms used to take place about once a year in the River Wye which runs alongside the chapel.

In the chapels the young women usually occupied the front seats, while the young men sat at the back. This gave them an opportunity to get out quickly at the end of the service and pick up the lady friend they wished to take home. We all wore bowler hats on Sundays, anything else would have been infra dig. Of course we were as fond of the girls then as young men are now, but the opportunities were more limited. No respectable girl would be allowed out more than one evening a week, except on Sundays and special occasions, but there were ways of circumventing such rules, and a chat could often be obtained by the back gate.

The chapels were the main source of social entertainment. During the winter months was held what was called a Christian Union. The two Glasbury chapels and Velindre chapel combined and held two entertainments in each chapel every winter. These always had to be arranged for the week of the full moon, so as to have moonlight on the way home. Our Three Cocks choir and band used to entertain frequently [as did the Glasbury handbell ringers, (Fig. 7.4)].

*Fig. 7.4 Glasbury handbell ringers in the early 20th century. R. Moy (second from the right) had a shop in Talgarth and was also a tower-bell ringer. The names of the other ringers are unknown. (Courtesy of the Glasbury History Group)*

*Fig. 7.5 The band that rang the first full peal on Talgarth bells, on 23 March 1907, and which included R. Moy, is commemorated on a wooden peal board and by photographs in the tower of St Gwendoline's church in Talgarth. (Photo by Colin Lewis)*

*Fig. 7.6  The first full peal by the local band on the church bells at Glasbury was rung on 27 September 1911, conducted by Leonard Lewis. The photograph shows (back row, left to right), The Honourable R.C. Devereux of Tregoyd, The Reverend Hugh H. Gibbon (vicar), Captain A. Glen Kidston of Gwernyfed Park, middle and front rows (in their shirtsleeves but not individually identified) the peal ringers: John N. Vizor, Arthur G. Arnold, Leonard Lewis, James P. Hyett, Edgar R. Jones, Thomas Turner. The two reserves, who did not ring, standing in their jackets on the front left and right respectively, were Edward Pugh and Thomas Vaughan. (Source: photograph in the Ringing Chamber of St Peter's Church, Glasbury)*

*Of the Glasbury peal ringers, according to the 1911 census, two were domestic gardeners – John Vizor, born in 1886 in Malmesbury in Wiltshire, and Arthur Arnold, born in 1888 in Suffolk. James Hyett, born in 1872, worked in the signal box of the Golden Valley Railway at Hay Station; he had learnt to ring at Norton Canon in Herefordshire. Leonard Lewis, born in 1878 in Clehonger in Herefordshire, was a police sergeant. Edgar Jones, born in Aberllynfi parish in 1890, was 'a farmer's son working on the land'. His parents farmed Great House (Fig. 7.7) in Aberllynfi, which was then part of the Gwernyfed Estate. The farmhouse, which lay near the road from Three Cocks village to Pipton on the way to Llyswen, has since been demolished. Jones was still ringing peals in 1951, when he seems to have lived in Bredwardine. The occupation of the sixth ringer (Thomas Turner) has not been established – there were six men of that name in Glasbury parish and it is not known which of them rang in the peal.[2]*

*Fig. 7.7 Great House, the home of Edgar Jones (see Fig. 7.6).*
*This house was in the part of the Gwernyfed Estate that was sold in 1922,*
*and was demolished after the end of the Second World War.*
*(From the Gwernyfed Sale Catalogue, 1922)*

The chapel anniversaries were great events. Both children and adults would take part and there were recitations and dialogues, solos, duets and quartets. There were also frequent tea parties, lectures, Christian Endeavour and Prayer meetings, and concerts. Only on rare occasions were outside artistes engaged; we made our own amusements! The Welsh Revival of 1904-5 reached Glasbury, and revival meetings were held there and in a private house in Pontithel.

Sometimes we would go further afield, to Pen yr heol (Fig. 8.2) and Maes yr Onnen (Figs. 7.8 & 7.9) chapels, or All Saints' Church, always on foot. We were not afraid of walking in those days. Three of our band used to play in the Talgarth Asylum dance band, travelling to Talgarth by train and returning on foot. On occasion I have walked home from Brecon at night. Llanthony Abbey and the monastery formed by an Anglican monk, Father Ignatius, were favourite long walks. Other amusements were the annual fairs at Hay, Talgarth, Builth and Brecon. Some hundreds of young people would travel by train to these events.

The local squire, Mr Wood of Gwernyfed, gave up his carriage horses in 1902 and purchased three motors to take their place. They were not very reliable, and it was a common occurrence for him to return home by train leaving the 'driver' to return with the car after repairs. Builth and Brecon were considered within a day's journey, but Hereford was too far and he would travel there by train.

The road from Pontithel to Glasbury and Hay used to be a beautiful country lane, with a rough surface, cart ruts, dirty and often muddy or dusty. Besides pedestrians, the

*Fig. 7.8  Maes yr Onnen chapel, near Ffynnon Gynydd.*
*(Postcard, courtesy of Mrs J. Thomas)*

*Fig. 7.9  The inside of Maes yr Onnen chapel in 2016.*
*(Photo by Logaston Press)*

only traffic on week days was an occasional farmer's trap, carts and wagons, and a peculiar shaped vehicle called a 'gambo', which was used for carting wood, and which I have never seen anywhere else. On Sundays it was practically pedestrians only, although there were crowds walking to and from the religious services. It was a matter of principle with most people not to take their horse out on Sundays. The hedges were high, and we could gather wild flowers and hedge nuts in season, and often used to run along dribbling a tennis ball.

Wages were low, farm labourers earning from 13s to 15s per week, with certain perquisites or privileges. On the other hand prices were low. The Pontithel Chemical Works employed about a dozen men at about 16s per week (Figs. 7.1 & 7.2). Cider was the main drink, perry and beer were also brewed at home. What was known as 'small beer' was also usually drunk, but was very weak. The stronger ale was only brought out on special occasions. Tea was not drunk more than once or twice a day.

The platelayers used to be given a week's holiday by the Cambrian Railways just before Christmas so that they could collect mistletoe, and I have been with them as far as Llowes and Clyro. Sometimes we would give some assistance with the farm work in return, and would usually be rewarded with a meal.

We used to have rare fun during the hay-making season, when the whole village would turn out to help. We used to go around the smallholdings helping one another, and where a horse and cart could not be obtained we would take the station four-wheeler, and with a few hurdles across to lengthen and widen it, would carry the hay on that.

Tramps were very common. The Chemical Works attracted them, as they were allowed to sleep by the fires. Most of them were genuine seekers after work, but there were also many regulars, such as 'Tommy Digger', a cheerful little fellow from Velindre. He would stay and chat for long enough if given a penny for half an ounce of twist tobacco. 'Old Tim' was a morose old fellow, and I never had much conversation with him, although I knew him well.

The newspapers circulating were *The Western Mail*, *The South Wales Daily News*, *The Brecon & Radnor Express* and *The Brecon County Times*. Very few people took a daily paper but the weeklies had a good circulation. The Station Master acted as newsagent.

Salmon poaching was very prevalent. The poachers used to light up the river to attract the fish, and as the only store of paraffin was at the station I am afraid the station paraffin was often used for this purpose. One Lad Porter was dismissed for stealing paraffin.

I only remember two 'great occasions'. One was the county council election in, I think, 1904, when Squire Wood was defeated by a Mr Jones of Llyswen, a Brecon solicitor. This was the result of Mr Balfour's Education Act and the opposition [to denominational schools] raised by Mr Lloyd George through the Welsh county councils. [The argument was over whether religion should be taught in schools on a non denominational line, and whether county council funding, therefore, should be withdrawn from any voluntarily run school that continued on denominational lines; the Liberal non denominational policy won the day.]

The other arose out of the visit to Birmingham Onion Fair of a married man and a married woman. This caused great scandal, and much gossip, culminating in a crowd of about one hundred gathering. Two effigies were made of a man and a woman, and the female effigy burnt outside the woman's house at Pontithel. A procession was then formed, headed by a man in a red soldier's uniform playing a bugle. Many of those taking part had blackened their faces.

When they burnt the second figure outside the man's house, it was found that the woman was inside. This resulted in stone throwing and almost a riot. Summonses were taken out against some of the ring-leaders, and crowds went to the Magistrates Court at Talgarth, all with an onion in their coat. Both sides were bound over to keep the peace, but a striking feature was that of the vicar of Glasbury, called to testify to the good character of the couple. He admitted in cross-examination that if they were guilty he would not disapprove of the methods used to punish them.

One more incident. The scene was a little cottage standing in a hollow adjoining the footpath from Three Cocks Station to Pipton. The cottager had died, and his widow, a poor old lady, was giving up the cottage and had a sale, and the first thing put up to auction was the old lady's cow. The price of the best cow at that time was about £20, the old lady's was one of the worst. The first bid was 2s 6d, then 5s and 7s 6d, and the auctioneer was trying hard to get a bid of 10s when a voice from the rear called out, £20. The bidder was a well-known farmer, and I shall never forget the hush that fell on the company. But the man's action changed the whole atmosphere of the sale, and instead of the old lady's effects being disposed of as so much rubbish, which I suppose it really was, they fetched a respectable sum. There was some human kindness about!

# 8  MEMORIES OF VELINDRE AND DISTRICT, THREE COCKS AND PART OF GLASBURY, 1880S-1960S

*Mary Kinsey in her later days lived near The Three Horse Shoes in Velindre and was related to many people on the Gwernyfed estate. The Revd E.T.D. Lewis, or so it is believed, encouraged her to write the following account of her memories.*

I attended Velindre School until I was 12 years old. I then went to Hampton Grammar School, in the Radnorshire side of Glasbury, until I was 14. [Hampton School stood on the right-hand side of the main road from Glasbury to Llowes, on the edge of Glasbury. It had been founded in the 1880s by a Mr W. Vaughan, and offered a Grammar-style education It closed in the early 1950s.] I was at that school in 1900, when the River Wye was frozen over. A horse and rider went across the river on the ice. One evening while the river was still frozen, Charlie and Annie Mitchell and myself walked across the river from Hampton School to Aberllynfi House, on the Breconshire side of the river. The Mitchells' father was a [game] keeper for Colonel Wood and the Gwernyfed Estate.

Now we come to Velindre [*circa* 1900], the 'home village' for the estate. The Stephens lived at Big Tyleglas, on the Talgarth side of Velindre. [This was a large farm]. Nearer Velindre was Little Tyleglas, where Price the cowman lived. Nearby was The Iron House [since destroyed] where a Keeper for Colonel Wood lived: he married the cook who used to be at Gwernyfed. Mr Thomas, the bailiff, lived in part of Old Gwernyfed, [as the old mansion, that had become Gwernyfed Farm in the latter years of the 19th century, became named once the new mansion of Gwernyfed Park had been built].

The Three Horseshoes Inn was located in Velindre, with Mr and Mrs George Price as licensees [and the inn is still there, beside the junction that serves the Cadarn Riding Centre]. They also kept a small grocery shop of small items. Next [to The Three Horseshoes Inn] was David Prothero, the blacksmith, with a man working with him, Parker Blackett. Then a little next to it a Mr and Mrs Russell. Mr Russell had served in the Boer War. Across the road [was] the Methodist Chapel and next a house where Mr Joe Russell lived, who was a postman.

At the top of the lane, near the brook, the first two houses were occupied by Mr and Mrs Stallard and Mr and Mrs Gore. Edward Gore was a roadman. Further down the lane lived my grandmother, Mrs Margaret Barret and her daughter Margaret, my mother's mother and her sister. Next door lived a Mrs Brown and two children. Further down lived Mr and Mrs Jones. Mr Jones was a carpenter for Colonel Wood. When Mr Jones passed away a Mr J. Price, carpenter and undertaker, went to live there with his family. Next lived John Price, who was a boot and shoe mender. The next house was Mrs Price, who was a dressmaker.

Coming back to the main road and over the river bridge lived Mr Evan Davies and family. He was a waggoner for Colonel Wood. Going around to the back was a yard where the saw-mills were located. The saws were worked from the brook that went through the yard. My father and Daniel Monkley were the ones who saw to all the timber being sawn for different purposes.

Come now to The Green, [where the church used to stand, see p.13]. Two people lived there: Mr J. Watkins, a boot and shoe repairer, and Mrs Olife, the governess when I was at Velindre School. She was succeeded by a Miss Z.A.H. Jones from up Llandrindod way.

[Past The Green, on the way towards Tregoyd] was Primrose Cottage where Mr and Mrs Walter Price lived. Mr Price was a carpenter and undertaker. When he passed away his son: David Walter, took over. After many years he was married to Miss Jones, the governess.

Now back to The Green and down to Clarence Cottage [by the road towards Glasbury (Fig. 4.14)]. Mr Williams and family lived there. He was a carpenter for Colonel Wood. Groesffordd (Fig. 8.1) belonged to the Old Gwernyfed Home Farm. Mr Ben Lloyd lived in one house and Mr Ben Pugh in the other, the first a waggoner and the second a cowman.

*Fig. 8.1 The Groesffordd, now occupied as one dwelling, but the homes of the Lloyd and Pugh families in the days of Mary Kinsey's memories. (Photo by Colin Lewis)*

On to Tregoyd Mill, first to Mr J. Phillips who owned a threshing machine and used to go round the farms far and wide. A Mr Cootes also lived there. He was a postman delivering letters as far as Lord Hereford [Tregoyd] and Velindre. Down over the brook was Tregoyd Mill where Mr J. Harris lived. He would grind the corn. He was a son of Mr and Mrs Harris who did the same at Three Cocks Mill.

Coming back from Tregoyd [Mill] to the Groesffordd, go up a little lane and you come on the main road to Hay and Talgarth. Going a little along that road for Hay you turn to the right and up that road for the Black Mountains. Newcourt Farm with Mr Alan Price, and Cwm-dau-nant are there. Further up that road you come to Penlan where the Phillips family lived. Mr Phillips was employed in the forestry with my father.

Across from there we come to the cottage where a Mr and Mrs Greenway lived, he was an animal slaughterer. Now we reach Trenewydd where, upon their marriages one son, John, went to Upper Cwmcadarn and one, William, to Lower Cwmcadarn.

Going back down to Velindre there were two houses facing the chapel, Daniel Monkley, employed in the saw mills in one, and Mr Arthur and Mr Mason, both [employed] on Colonel Wood's estate. Up to the Clyres [where] lived a Mr Price who was a tailor, and father for G. Price from The Three Horseshoes. Next door a Mrs Thomas lived and her daughter, Gwen, who later married a Mr G. Didwood who also worked on the estate.

Over the brook was Brook Cottage where Mr and Mrs William James Jones used to live. Mr Jones was a mason for Colonel Wood; his nick-name was 'Jack Baco'. He had a daughter and a son whose nickname was 'Billy Baco'. Back over the brook and up the hill on the right was Dan y common [a farm]. Back down the hill and turn right past Velindre School [and] one comes to a cottage called Pant y gollen, where Watkin lived. He was a forester for Colonel Wood.

Below Pant y gollen lay Lower Cwmcadarn, where William Stephens lived. He later farmed Big Tyleglas. [Beyond] Lower Cwmcadarn was where lived a farmer named Mr John Jones, who was a breeder of Hereford cattle. He entered small shows and often judged at them. He was on his way to judge at some show when he collapsed at Paddington Station after getting off the train. John Stephens then farmed at Upper Cwmcadarn for years, and his widow kept the farm on for a while after his death. They had one daughter who took up nursing, the last I heard [she] had made it up to matron. Her mother sold the farm and went to live in Talgarth. I have now remembered who lived at Upper Cwmcadarn before John Stephens bought it: A Mrs Thomas and her two sons from Cwmdu bought Cwmcadarn. She had one daughter, who married David Greenow, a son of Philip Greenow the Noyadd. They went to live at Pentre wen, Llyswen. After Mrs Thomas had passed [away], David Charles took over the farm until it went on fire [in the 1960s] when he was drinking and smoking. Lloyd James tried to save him, but failed.

I think I will go back to Maes y lade, where a Mr and Mrs Jones lived when we lived at Cefn y Waun. [They were followed by] some people with the name of Wooley and then Leonard (Jacko) James. [Vernon James, one of the sons, developed an agricultural and road making/earth moving business and married Margaret Davies (née Holtam), who had been brought-up in Box Cottage. Margaret had initially married John Davies of Heol y gaer, a Leading Seaman in the Royal Navy who was drowned trying to save lives after a liberty boat disaster. She had been a dental nurse in Brecon before her marriage. Vernon and Margaret lived in a council house in Glasbury before building Brook Haven in Three Cocks. Margaret succeeded Eric Smith as organist at St Peter's Church, while Vernon became one of the churchwardens.]

On now to Cwm wnt, in ruins many years, people by name of Curran, with two boys: George and John, [who] were in Velindre School when I was there.

[On] to Blaina, I can't remember the name of the people there, then to the Noyadd, then to the Llanarch where my father was born. Down below they used to say an old lady lived and she used to wear three underskirts, all below the other. Next, up to Bryn dwy nant, where Powells lived, two brothers and a sister, the one brother was a minister. Then to Cwm bach where a Mr and Mrs Griffiths lived. Their eldest sons, Johnny and Tommy, were in school with me.

Now up to Pen yr heol Chapel (Fig. 8.2), where there was an Anniversary Service one Sunday every year. The children were reciting at the afternoon and evening services. I used to recite at both. After the afternoon service we used to go back to Cefn y Waun and mother used to take people who had come a long way and give them tea and then go back for the evening service. On the Monday we used to have another service where tea was prepared for everyone who came to it.

Then we come to Pen yr heol Cottage and down to the pool hewn out of rock where members of the chapel were baptised. My mother and I went one Sunday morning when there were 20 baptised at the Dipping Pool. After the dipping we went to a house where

*Fig. 8.2 Pen yr heol Baptist Chapel as it was in 2016,*
*with a converted stable in the right foreground. (Photo by Colin Lewis)*

the members had a hot drink and changed into dry clothing: the last [baptism there] that I remember was when there was snow on the ground.

[Beyond] the Dipping Pool were [farms] named Blaen di Gedi, the Upper and Lower Island and a cottage called Cock a Lofty nearer the Black Mountains. Over the mountain by Lord Hereford's Knob [the unfenced land below the Gospel Pass] used to be called the Blaenburch [Blaen Bwlch] where Philip Greenow was mountain shepherd for Lord Hereford. Later he went to live at the Noyadd. Down the mountain to Capel y ffin and on to the monastery where Father Ignatius resided with Brothers David and Matthew and Sisters Winifred, Mary and Martha. There were two peacocks at the monastery.

My mother, two friends and I went [to the monastery] twice a year, in May and August. We would walk all the way to a service in the morning and then be given lunch, gentlemen and boys in one room and ladies and girls in another. It was a super lunch! After that we went to afternoon service and then were given tea and refreshments before going home. There used to be a crowd of folk there in those days.

There is a square of ground in the corner of the monastery where Father Ignatius was supposed to have seen the Virgin appear. The railing was still around there when some relatives wanted to go there to see the monastery, that was 22 years ago we went [probably *circa* 1940]. All the monastery was in ruins, some part a farmer had for his flocks. Father Ignatius was buried there.

[Beyond the monastery, in Capel y ffin, was] the little church, I should say the smallest in the world. The pews would only seat about two people, and a little organ and pulpit, quite a novelty. Across the brook was a farm and the Baptist chapel.

Coming back through Capel y ffin you come to Lord Hereford's land on the right, and Colonel Wood had part of the mountain on the left for his sheep. My uncle was shepherd for him. He lived at a place called Wern frank and in later years the Stephens, Tyleglas, had it for a time. One of the sons lived there but a sad thing was that he hanged himself there – I think his name was Eddie.

I will now go to Three Cocks and Glasbury. Gwernyfed Park, where Colonel and Mrs Wood lived, was here [near Three Cocks]. They had two sons, and a daughter who married Mr Hore-Ruthven and had Old Gwernyfed modernised and lived there. Colonel Wood used to have a lot of deer in the park. The butler lived at The Lodge. [Back towards Three Cocks was] the house Mr Nusser [? probably Nunn] built with the aid of his two daughters. He was a schoolmaster at Boughrood School. Then came Park View where a Baptist minister lived. Then Waltham cottages where my father and mother lived in the days when he had retired from the forestry. Mr and Mrs Price, who had been a clerk and caretaker of St Peter's Church before my Uncle Jones took over the duties, [lived next door]. My aunt used to clean the church and did so until they passed away. My uncle served in the Boer War, he used to live at Aberllynfi Cottage. On The Green [in Three Cocks] lived the Reckitts who used to keep a dairy farm and used to supply milk to most of the people. In the house down by the brook the Williamses lived. Mr Williams worked on the Midland Railway line.

The Three Cocks Hotel was up the road, where a Mr and Mrs Wilcocks were licensed. Later a Mr and Mrs Reading were there. I don't know who took over from them. [Across the stream from the hotel was] the mill where Mr and Mrs J. Harris lived and used to do

Fig. 8.3 *The funeral of Captain Glen Kidston, 1931. His father, Archibald Glen Kidston (1871-1913), of a Glasgow shipping family, had rented Gwernyfed Park from Colonel Wood as a sporting estate. Archibald Glen Kidston was very generous to St Peter's Church in Glasbury and to the locality. He donated the fine organ that is still used at St Peter's and paid for an organ chamber to be built for it. He also paid for a glass screen to be installed in the archway between the ringing chamber and the nave, and for a set of ten hand-bells for the ringers. He also donated a challenge shield to be rung for annually by members of the Hereford Diocesan Guild of Bell Ringers. His male employees were expected to play cricket on a ground that he laid-out in the park. On Sundays they were also expected to sing in the church choir and/or ring the bells! Archibald Glen Kidston died while being operated on for cancer in 1913. His coffin was carried to St Peter's by 11 of the gamekeepers from the estate and was followed by family mourners and 35 servants. His son's funeral was even more spectacular as this photograph shows. (Photograph courtesy of Mrs June Thomas)*

all the grinding for the farmers. Across [from them] lived a Mr Minton and Mr Woods who were gardeners, like my uncle, for Colonel Wood and then for Captain Kidston when he [leased] Gwernyfed Park. [Captain Kidston moved to Gwernyfed in 1908, he died in 1913.]

My uncle went to live at Church House [beside St Peter's churchyard] and supervised the planting of the [daffodil] bulbs that Captain Kidston had given for the churchyard [sometime in the period 1908-1913.] My uncle was one of the bearers of Glen Kidston, the great aeroplane expert. [He flew the first air mail from Britain to South Africa (Cape Town) in 1931 but crashed into the Drakensberg on the return flight. His body was brought back

*Fig. 8.4 Pupils of Coed y Bolen (Glasbury), Velindre, and Ffynnon Gynydd Church Schools assembled on the Lower Common by Coed y Bolen School during the Diamond Jubilee celebrations of 1897. Part of Penlan, the home of Mr Butcher the land agent for the Gwernyfed Estate, can be seen in the background.*
*(Source, Velindre School archive, courtesy of Mr Glen Smith)*

to Glasbury where he is buried near his father in St Peter's churchyard.] I took the children to the Common [which overlooks the churchyard] to see the funeral (Fig. 8.3).

The Revd H. Fitzgibbon [Hugh Gibbon, Fig. 4.24] was vicar of St Peter's for years [1883-1926]. He christened me and all my children bar one who was christened in Talgarth at the time she was born. I had ten children, eight girls and two boys. Both the boys served in the Second World War. My eldest son, Athelstan, had joined the Royal Air Force after he had finished his apprenticeship when he was 17. My two eldest daughters were married in St Peter's: Gwen and Kathleen, and three of my grandsons were christened there.

[I can remember] Queen Victoria's [Diamond] Jubilee (1897), which was a great day (Fig. 8.4). There were two tents with all refreshments. One tent was on the Common [by Glasbury School (Coed y Bolen)] and one in Mr Charles Butcher's field [at Penlan]. He was the land agent for Colonel Wood then. There were a lot of other things there. I think we had to go to the Service in the Church first and then to a Reception where everyone had a lovely time.

[John Jones of Upper Cwmcadarn] had got up a choir of girls and boys of the village and we used to have practices once or twice a week. Mr Tom Morgan our postman, who used to deliver mail round Velindre, Cefn y Waun, Maes y lade and up as far as Noyadd and Trenewydd, used to help train the choir. We used to have concerts in the school at Velindre and the choir used to go there to give their services sometimes.

Once or twice at the Methodist Chapel there were competitions. I won a certificate once which was for Scripture. The last concert we did was at the school. I recited the Burial of Moses and Mr Morgan gave the rendering of the Holy City. He also had a prize. The choir ended with 'Adieu, kind friends, Adieu', as it was the last of the choir as Mr Jones was moving to a farm near Hay called The Sheephouse. I think the proceeds of that [concert] went to improve the school. We all missed the choir very much.

# 9    POSTSCRIPT

According to parochial records, in 1762 sermons at St Peter's church in Glasbury took place alternately in English and Welsh.[1] By 1807, when the Wood family were landlords of Gwernyfed, services (presumably including sermons) were all in English.[2] In 1828 it was stated that Communion was held only five times a year at St Peter's.[3] In 2016 almost every service at St Peter's was Communion, contrary to a tradition that probably extended back to the 16th century, when the bishops of Wales and Hereford were charged with publishing a Bible in Welsh so that people could hear the Word of God in their own language.

Welsh continued to be a common language in the Gwernyfed area until at least the mid-19th century, but it was not then the language of the well-nigh feudal landlord family and faded away under their influence. The language is still spoken in the area by a few people. Elyned Hore-Ruthven makes no mention of Welsh in *A Victorian Childhood*. She was essentially a privileged English girl growing up in Wales, rather than a Welsh speaking Welshwoman (albeit from Herefordshire) like the bride whom Harry Williams brought to Gwernyfed in 1605 and who was honoured with a poetic bardic welcome, in the Welsh of this benevolent border-land area.

When the first of her former pupils from Velindre School graduated in 1985, Mrs B.W. Lewis, who was then headmistress of that school (Fig. 9.1), considered that even semi-feudalism had ended at Gwernyfed. Her predecessor as headmistress, Mrs D.W. Price, was something of a poet and produced a 48 verse description of the leading people of the Velindre area for the Silver Jubilee celebrations for King George V in the village in 1935. In 1976 for the opening of Velindre Village Hall on the former site of Velindre church, she wrote a further poem. These poems are shown on Appendices 2 and 3.

Gwernyfed is best known in the second decade of the 21st century as the home of an excellent secondary school. The school opened in 1950 and was then housed in the mansion of Gwernyfed Park. The school, which still centres on the mansion and its gardens, has gone from strength to strength and at the end of 2016 Gwernyfed High School had 450 pupils aged from 11 to 18 and over 30 teachers. It has been categorised by the Welsh Government as a 'Green School' – the highest educational category for schools in Wales – and in recent years many students have gone up to Oxford, Cambridge and other excellent universities.

As befits a secondary school in a rural area, Gwernyfed High School offers a vocational agricultural course, those successfully completing this course being qualified to proceed to agricultural college.

*Fig. 9.1. The teaching staff and pupils of Velindre School in 1962.*
*Back row, left to right: Mrs Morwen Pugh (teacher), Michael Jones, Michael James,*
*Marilyn Vaughan, Gwyneth Powell, Joyce Jones, Christopher Hobson, Charlie Fuller,*
*Philip Jones, Colin Vaughan, Mrs Barbara W. Lewis (headmistress).*
*Front row, left to right: John Roberts, Alvin Powell, Richard James, Gillian Abberley,*
*Janice James, Pauline Price, Beverley Hobson, Paul Price, Elvin Griffiths, Michael Price,*
*Shirley James, John Price. (Photo from Velindre School archives, courtesy of Mr Glen Smith.*
*The School was closed in 1993)*

The school hosts many local clubs and events and is a focal point for a wide geographical area. Gwernyfed Rugby Club, for example, which is one of the leading community clubs in Wales, was founded in 1965 by two teachers from the School: David Knapp and Bernard Altmeyer. A lesser known example of this community engagement was the involvement of another teacher, Fran Bateman, in teaching change ringing to local bell-ringers until she injured herself in a sporting accident.

Over a thousand years have passed since the native Welsh rulers of the Gwernyfed region were defeated in battle by Norman invaders. Over 400 years have gone since David Williams, a Welsh lawyer, purchased Gwernyfed mansion and founded a landlord dynasty. Gwernyfed is no longer a landlord estate but remains as a beautiful, fertile, welcoming region, under the shadow of the Black Mountains.

# Appendix 1 — Horse-breeding & travelling stallions
by Colin Lewis

In chapter 6, Thomas Perks does not explain how his grandmother ran her horse-breeding system or describe the stallions she used for her mares. In her time there was a well-developed system of travelling stallions in England and Wales, initially operating under private enterprise. In the 1830s, in Scotland, a number of heavy-horse hiring societies were established. Each society hired one or more stallions for the breeding season, and the stallion owners entered into a contract to travel the stallion/s within the district covered by the society. Each stallion was led by a groom who, with the horse, walked along an advertised route. Mares that were in season could be brought to one of the stopping places on the stallion's route, and, for a fee, would be served there and then by the stallion.

The first non-ephemeral heavy-horse hiring society to be established south of the Scottish border was the Montgomeryshire District Entire Horse Association, founded in 1877.[1] By the late 19th and early 20th centuries Britain and Ireland were divided into horse-breeding areas served by heavy-horse hiring societies, as shown for England and Wales on Figure A.1. Prior to the establishment of hiring societies, stallions were travelled privately by their owners, often along advertised and regular routes. Mrs Probert's mares may initially have been bred to such privately travelled stallions, each of which was normally expected to serve at least 40 mares per breeding season: some served over 100!

In her later years Mrs Probert may have bred her mares to society or other premium stallions. Premium stallions, of various breeds and types, included those approved and financially supported by the Hunters' Improvement Society, the Royal Agricultural Society of England, the Royal Commission on Horse Breeding, the Board of Agriculture and Fisheries, the War Office, and by other such bodies.

The route followed each week by the Glasbury Shire Horse Society's stallion between the 1920s and 1970s is shown on Figure A.2. This route, with the scheduled stopping times at various centres, was advertised on cards that were circulated in the area covered by the society. Figure A.3 shows a typical Shire Horse stallion being displayed by his leader on the show-grounds near Brecon in the period 1936-8.

In addition to heavy horse stallions there were Welsh Cob and Thoroughbred stallions travelling the Velindre area in the 19th and 20th centuries under governmental breeding schemes, one of which is shown on Figure A.4.

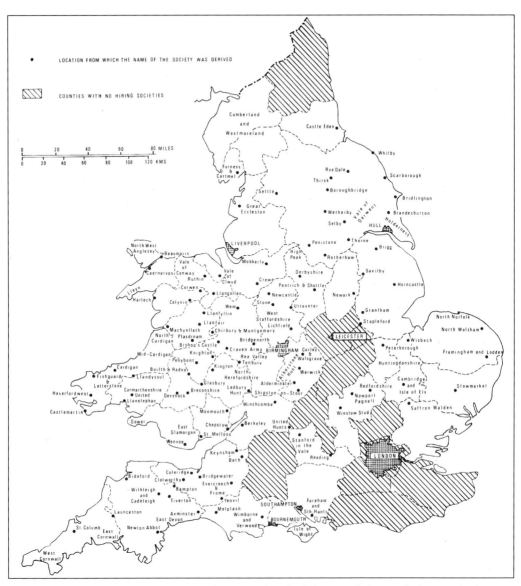

*Fig. A.1 Heavy horse and other stallions used to be led around the roads during the horse breeding season, normally April until July, and served mares that were in season and brought to them from farms and other establishments. The breeders were charged for the services of the stallions. From 1877 onwards draught stallions of approved quality were increasingly under contract to heavy horse hiring societies. In 1914, in order to improve the quality of draught horses, the Board of Agriculture began to issue grants to each such society that was approved by the Board. These grants continued to be paid until the Second World War. In 1939 there were four approved heavy horse hiring societies in Breconshire: the Glasbury Shire Horse Society; the Breconshire Shire Horse Society; the Devynock Shire Horse Society; and the Builth and Radnor Shire Horse Society. This map shows the location of all the approved heavy horse hiring societies in England and Wales in 1939. Gwernyfed was sited within the area travelled by the Glasbury Shire Horse Society's stallion.[2]*

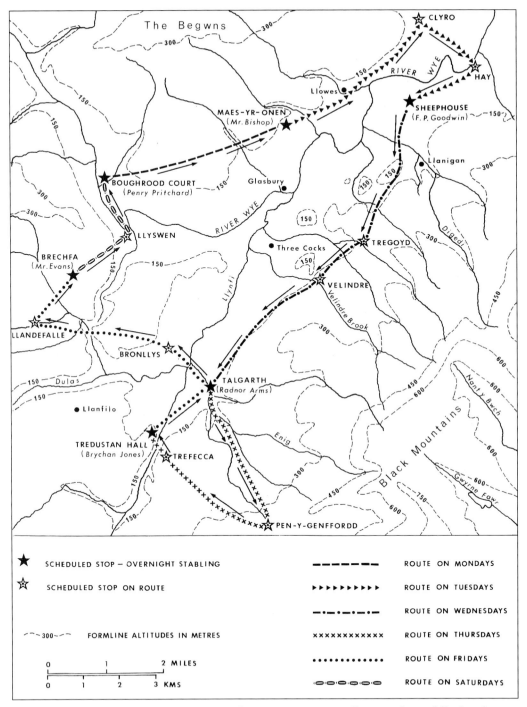

Fig. A.2 *The route of the Glasbury Shire Horse Society stallion in the middle decades of the 20th century. For much of that period the stallion was based at Boughrood Court and visited the Velindre/Gwernyfed area weekly.*[3]

*Fig. A.3  Mr Bill Evans of Glasbury displaying W. Milner's grey Shire Horse stallion,
which he led during the horse breeding seasons of 1936-38.[4]*

*Fig. A.4  In 1937 a Welsh Cob, Paith Flyer II, owned by Mr Jones of Bailey Merdy, Brilley,
visited Velindre once a fortnight. The horse was led by Nicholas Jones, seen here on the left
riding the stallion at a local show.[5]*

During the 1930s, with increasing mechanisation of farms, the need for horses diminished. As a result fewer mares were sent to stallions. In 1937, since there had been so little demand for the services of the stallion in the previous year, the route travelled by Paith Flyer II, the War Office Premium Welsh Cob stallion for the area, was divided between Breconshire and Radnorshire on a fortnightly basis, as shown on Figure A.5.

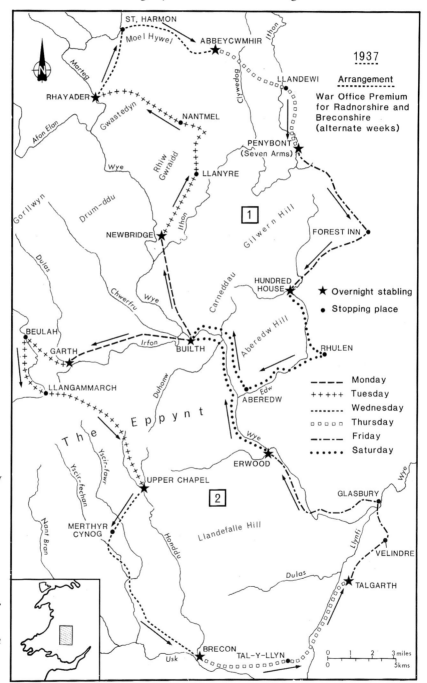

Fig. A.5 The route followed by Paith Flyer II in the breeding season of 1937. Alternate weeks in Radnorshire (1) and Breconshire (2). Velindre and the Gwernyfed area were included in the Breconshire route.[6]

*Fig. A.6 Kerry Dorothy, a quality work horse mare, 16.2 hands high, from the Gwernyfed
Estate area, photographed in the 1930s. (From the author's collection)*

A quality work-horse mare from the Gwernyfed Estate area in the 1930s, Kerry Dorothy
(Fig. A. 6), probably resembled some of the heavy horses bred and employed by Mrs Probert
over 60 years earlier.

# APPENDIX 2    VELINDRE JUBILEE (6 MAY 1935)

*by* Z.A.H. Jones

Velindre village, so they say,
Will never be so jolly and gay,
As it will be on the 5th of May,
       All for the Jubilee.

The pub will be full, the beer will flow,
And Price to the cellar oft will go,
We'll have a real good royal show,
       All for the Jubilee.

Phillips, The Mill, and John Price Jones,
Are busy oiling their stiffened bones,
And practising three-legged race over stones,
       All for the Jubilee.

William Stephens will come to the show,
He has no liking for going below,
"Down to Glasbury", he says, "some day we'll go";
       But not for this Jubilee.

Jim Price is sorry he can't run;
He says the rheumatism will spoil his fun;
But if he can't manage, he'll send his son
       To run for the Jubilee.

Evan Davies says: "Now, young Squire Price,
You're just the right age, and about the right size;
I remember running and winning a prize
       At the last Jubilee".

Then up comes John Jones and tells them all
He's afraid if he runs, he might have a fall.
But he's practising jumping his garden wall,
       All for the Jubilee.

Along comes Billie [Arrowsmith] with serious face,
He runs with Jim Gore in the Bachelor's race,
"If I don't win," says Jim, "I'll sure get a place
       In the race at the Jubilee".

Davey and Wilfred and Williams are tall,
But for running they are no good at all,
They cover too much of the ground when they fall,
       All in the Jubilee.

Morris,[1] Gwernyfed, is lending the ground,
Giving his blessing as well as a pound;
Could a better fellar than that be found
       For any Jubilee?

[Ernest] Price, Pentwyn, says "I'll join with you,
But there's money to get and a lot to do,
And if you are short you'll be in a stew
       On the day of the Jubilee".

Farr will be in the tug-of-war,
The kids will have swings and a nice see-saw,
And they'll shout until they get lock-jaw
       At Velindre Jubilee.

Jim Meredith will take his place
With Price, the Newcourt, in the sack race;
They'll show you how to go the pace
       At Velindre Jubilee.

Duncan will come from the Dipping Pool,
And dance the polka with Miss Jones, The School,
And everybody will act the fool
       At Velindre Jubilee.

Bert Harris will come with his snow-white mare,
And William, his father, will also be there;
They'll all do their best, and all take a share
      In Velindre Jubilee.

Davey Jones will come with some persuasion
To celebrate the great occasion,
To attend will be a great temptation,
      The gay Jubilee.

Davey Thomas will run with Sammy Gore –
I expect these two have run before;
And Sammy will laugh and make us roar
      At Velindre Jubilee.

[James] Abberley's policy's safe and sound.
He says, "Let's stick to Velindre ground,
No better place can ever be found
      To hold the Jubilee".

And Tommy, his son, says, "Yes, oh, rather!
I'm sure I think the same as father;
I'll run until I'm all of a lather
      At Velindre Jubilee".

Davey and Johnny Greenow'll come down
To have a stroll round Velindre town,
And Sally will have a nice new gown
      For Velindre Jubilee.

Alf Powell says, "I quite agree,
Velindre is the place for me,
And George and I'll go on the spree
      For Velindre Jubilee."

Says [Lewis] Price, The Cefn, "My neighbour Bill
Can't walk too far, it makes him ill,
So to Velindre we'll come from off the hill,
      To spend our Jubilee.

Rhys Lloyd says to his neighbour, Brown,
"We may as well be in London Town
For they 're going to spend over twenty pounds
      At Velindre Jubilee.

Up speaks Prosser, "Well, I'm so glad-
To go from Velindre would be sad.
A good time here we've always had
      So 'Three Cheers for the Jubilee'."

[Ernest] Griffiths, Tre-newydd, and James, Maes-y-lade,
Hope preparations will not be delayed.
They feel too long at home they've stayed,
      But they'll come to the Jubilee.

Eddie Phillips [Tregoyd Mill] will put his thresher away,
He can't be bothered with work that day,
He'll have a day off on the 6th of May,
      All for the Jubilee.

[Harold] Jones, The Village [Tregoyd], says, "I've no dou
There'll be a good time, and we'll all turn out,
And some of the blokes will be 'up the spout'
      On the night of the Jubilee."

Christy Morris came down and said one day,
"I'll give ten bob at Velindre to stay,
I wish I'd a son who could run that day
      All for the Jubilee".

[Edward] Watkins will run in the Veterans race,
And [Edward] Gore will also compete in the chase;
We'll see all the old uns going the pace
      At Velindre Jubilee.

[George] Smart[2] will plan all the races you know
And be M.C. for the evening show;
He'll tell the bugler when to blow
      At Velindre Jubilee.

[Claude] Foxlow comes along with the rest
And he says he's willing to do his best,
With his flags we'll have the village dressed,
      All for the Jubilee.

We'll also be glad to welcome Seal,
And we hope quite well that he'll feel,
And share with us our festive meal,
      At Velindre Jubilee.

Howell Price, down from the Lane,
Says he hopes it will not rain,
Then we'll all meet once again
   At Velindre Jubilee.

Davey and Oswald [Thomas], Cwmcadarn, will come,
And [Ernest] Griffiths, Pencoed, will join in the fun,
The hedging and ploughing all is done
   Before the Jubilee.

Greenow, Cwmdynant, says, "I'll come,
But I've plenty of work to do at home;
I've never been a chap to roam,
   But I'll come to the Jubilee."

Turner, Cwmbach, will leave his farm,
To enjoy himself will be no harm.
When the burglar comes, we'll sound the alarm
   At Velindre Jubilee.

Joseph Amphlett, Well done, Joe!!
Says to Glasbury he won't go,
Declares we'll have a tip-top show
   At Velindre Jubilee.

[James] Gore and [Edward] Hamer, so they say,
Will put their spades away that day,
There'll be plenty to eat and nothing to pay
   At Velindre Jubilee.

Mrs Seaborne will also take her place
In the egg-and-spoon or the needle race,
She'll tell you she could go at a pace
   At the last Jubilee.

Gittoes, Penlan, has given his share.
And Watkins, The Blaina, will also be there;
'Twill be a very good affair,
   Velindre Jubilee.

Eddie Price, Tregoyd, they say,
May find a bride round here that day.
So "Here's luck to him on the 6th of May
   At Velindre Jubilee."

Alan Price is coming to our show
Though his thoughts are by nature below
But down there he intends to go,
   After the Jubilee.

Harold Jones, Cwmclend, Well Done!
Will come and bring his Jubilee son;
And [Peter] James, Pentrecoch, will join in the fun
   At Velindre Jubilee.

Eckley will come from Windsor that day,
And [George] Harris, Cefn y Waun, will say,
"I really could not stay away
   From Velindre Jubilee."

Llewelyn Greenow, so they say,
Will bring his bride along that day.
Now, who is going to be Queen of the May
   At Velindre Jubilee?

Beef and ham and cherry cake
Stuff that will give you an awful ache.
If you eat more than you ought to take
   At Velindre Jubilee.

All we want is a shave and a wash,
Plenty of "grub" and plenty of "splosh",
And our celebrations will be "posh"
   For Velindre Jubilee.

So the people gather round and say,
"I hope the sun shines on the 6th of May,
For the kids to sing and the band to play
   At Velindre Jubilee."

1 Morris was the farm manager at Old Gwernyfed
2 George Smart was a gamekeeper from Tregoyd

# APPENDIX 3     WELCOME TO VELINDRE

*by* Mrs Z.A.H. Price (*née* Jones)

Welcome to Velindre! And to our Village Hall!
This is a great occasion and we welcome one and all,
Now Velindre Village has a Hall we're proud to call our own.

We've waited many years, and struggled all alone.
We lacked a room to hold a concert or a dance,
Or a meeting place for younger folk, who never had a chance.

However, when we got awake, some of the people knew
They had to face so many snags, they knew not what to do.
But we started in a little way and their efforts swiftly grew
And soon we had support, not only from the few,
Carol Perry and Margaret Evans began to blaze the trail
By clearing rubbish, and to work they did not fail.

A good committee was formed with Wilfred Stephens at its head
To consider all the pro's and con's, and they were wisely led.
Elvet Jones and Clive James were very soon in action,
And Graham Sinclair (Treasurer) gave every satisfaction.
Mrs Gwyneth Williams (Secretary) worked so very well,
And Mrs Vera Griffiths (Vice Chairman) you can tell
Never missed a chance to get donations or a prize.
Cooking and dressing dolls of every kind and size.
With Mrs Gordon Powell they travelled many miles
Begging good donations, and returning thanks and smiles.
Mrs Elvet Jones and Mrs [Julysia (Julie)] Sinclair worked hard behind the scenes.
They helped their husbands all the time, and we all know what that means.

Mesdames [Joan (Mrs Sid)] Price and [Rose] Hobby, Forty, [Lily] Jones, and [Eleanor] Reid
Made catering a pleasure, and helped at every "feed".
They gave refreshments, got the prizes and each member would contrive
To help at every function, coffee morning or whist drive.

112

The Committee swiftly got to work to find the needful cash,
With Miss [Gwenllian] Phillips giving good advice on grants and spending cash.

Gordon Powell and Ernest Griffiths kept the home fires burning
To let their wives go begging and often late returning.
Clive and Margaret [James] never failed to help at all occasions
To help the organisers do the decorations.
Emlyn Hargest lent his field to hold a barbeque,
And Mrs Hargest always supported every social "do".

Mrs Beetham (Old Gwernyfed) with cheerful smile but little warning,
Was always helpful fixing up a coffee morning.
Another helpful lady, Mrs [Elsie] Slater, lent her home for meetings, too.
For without a room or fire, what could the Committee do?
Mrs Humphrey [Irene] Webb has a cupboard down at Hay
And Velindre knows she's generous, and gave scores of cakes away.
With her husband Humphrey, she'd see they'd nothing lack,
While he was very generous and gave our Hall its plaque.
The Committee always had advice from our Vicar, Mayor of Brecon,
Who, with Vernon James, are useful men we reckon.
The officials on the job were helpful and quite fair,
They gave some very useful tips to work with greatest care.
Our neighbours from Llanigon were generous with donations.
'Tis good to know we have good friends in such a situation.
Everything progressed so well, the contractors did not shirk,
They did not stop to stand and talk, but kept plodding at their work.

The Committee had to face the fact that they were in a plight,
They could not further act, without a suitable site.
What we need to proceed was a generous friend.
And if you work and do the right, 'twill come right in the end.

Next, the late Reg Parry, with a heart so kind and good,
Remembered the good wife he'd lost, and told us that he would
Gladly give the site they begged, and which he did then name
And with them to accept it, as a tribute to her name.

What a splendid gift it was! And how grateful we should be
Our troubles now were growing less and how happy we could be
One or two were very anxious about a Right of Way
And Right of Access which would surely cause delay.
We then appealed to Mrs. Luddington, the Lady of the Manor,
Who responded like her family, in their usual gracious manner,
She granted them the rights they sought and readily gave all
For the sake of Old Gwernyfed and Velindre Village Hall.
So today we stand together, we've struggled and we've won,
And to thank our kind supporters for the good work they have done.

# REFERENCES

Many of the main characters in the Historical Introduction have entries in *The history of Parliament: the House of Commons* and/or in Wikipedia. The latter source is not always reliable, but it has been consulted and deemed acceptable for the present purpose: to provide readers with a general introduction to the remainder of this book. Individual references to Wikipedia entries and to pedigrees given in such sources as *Cracroft's Peerage* are not listed hereunder.

**Notes**
1. Duncan, D.E., 1998 *The Calendar*, Fourth Estate (1998), pp.309-11.

**Chapter 1**
1. Shaw, W.A., *The Knights of England etc.*, Sherratt and Hughes (1906).
2. Remfry, P., *The Castles of Breconshire*, Logaston Press (1999).
3. Dawson, M.L., 'Notes on the history of Glasbury', *Archaeologia Cambrensis*, **18**, (1918), pp.6-34, 279-319.
4. Jones, T., *History of the County of Brecknock*, George North printer and seller, and J. Booth, seller, London (1800 and 1809).
5. Briggs, C.S. and Lloyd, N., 'Old Gwernyfed: an Elizabethan garden in history and poetry', *Gerddi*, **4**, (2005-6), pp.7-35.
6. Dawson, op. cit.
7. AHD, 'Williams, David (d.1613), of Gwernyfed, Aberllynfi, Brec, Serjeants' Inn, London and Kingston House, Kingston Bagpuze, Berks' in *The history of Parliament: the House of Commons, 1558-1603*, Boydell and Brewer (1981).
8. Jones, S.R. and Smith, J.T., 'The houses of Breconshire', *Brycheiniog*, **10**, (1964), p.89.

**Chapter 2**
1. Bowen, L., 'Williams, Sir Henry (c.1579-80-1636), of Gwernyfed, Aberllynfi, Brec.'in *The history of Parliament: the House of Commons, 1604-1629*, Thrush, A. and Ferris, J. P. (eds), Cambridge University Press (2010).
2. ibid.
3. See Richardson, R.E., *Mistress Blanche, Queen Elizabeth I's confidante*, Logaston Press (2007).
4. ibid.
5. Williams, G.J., 'Croeso y Wernyfed', *Llên Cymru*, **8**, (1964-5), pp.81-3.
6. Richardson, op. cit.
7. Bowen, op. cit
8. Briggs, C.S. and Lloyd, N., 'Old Gwernyfed: an Elizabethan garden in history and poetry', *Gerddi*, **4**, (2005-6), pp.7-35.
9. Lewis, C.A., *Hunting in Ireland: an historical and geographical analysis*, J.A. Allen (1975).
10. Briggs and Lloyd, op. cit.
11. Johnston, D.C., *Iolo Gôch: poems*, Gomer Press (1993).
12. Jones, T., *History of Brecknockshire*, Blissett, Davies and Co., (1898 edition), p.351
13. Peate, I.C., *The Welsh House*, Hugh Evans (1946). (Republished Llanerch Press).
14. Jones, S.R. and Smith, J.T., 'The houses of Breconshire', *Brycheiniog*, **10**, (1964), p.89.

15. Hibbard, G.R., 'The country house poem of the seventeenth century', *Journal of the Warburg and Courtauld Institutes*, **19**, (1956), pp.159-174.

16. Lewis, J. Saunders, *A School of Welsh Augustans; being a study in English influence in Welsh literature during part of the 18th century*, Hughe (1924); and 'Dafydd Nanmor', in *Meistri'r Canrifoedd: Ysgrifau ar Hanes Llenyddirth Gymreig gan Saunders Lewis*, Gruffydd, R.C. (ed), Cardiff (1973).

17. www.britishlistedbuildings/Llangoed, consulted 8/4/2016.

18. Dawson, M.L., 'Notes on the history of Glasbury', *Archaeologia Cambrensis*, **18**, (1918), p.287.

19. Helms, M.W. and Ferris, J.P., 1983 'Williams, Sir Henry 2nd Bt. (*c.*1635-1666), of Gwernyfed, Aberllynfi, Brec' in *The history of Parliament: the House of Commons, 1660-1690*, Henning, B.D. (ed), Boydell and Brewer.

20. Dawson, op, cit., p.288.

21. ibid, p.290.

22. Williams, J., 'Some particulars concerning the Parish of Glasbury', *Archaeologia Cambrensis*, Fourth Series, no. **4**, (1870), pp.306-323.

23. Hayton, D.W., 'Williams, Sir Edward (1659-1721), of Gwernyfed, Aberllynfi, Brec' in *The history of Parliament: the House of Commons, 1690-1715*, Hayton, D., Cruikshank, E., and Handley, S. (eds), Boydell and Brewer (2002).

24. Rowlands, E., 1983 'Williams, Sir Thomas, 1st Bt (*c.*1621-1712), of Elham, Kent' in *The history of Parliament: the House of Commons 1660-1690*, Henning, B.D. (ed), Boydell and Brewer.

25. www.coflein.gov.uk/pdf/CPG3.

## Chapter 3

1. Hayton, D.W., 'Williams, Sir Edward (1659-1721), of Gwernyfed, Aberllynfi, Brec'. in *The history of Parliament: the House of Commons, 1690-1715*, Hayton, D., Cruikshank, E., and Handley, S. (eds), Boydell and Brewer (2002).

2. Lewis, C.A., *Henry Williams the Glasbury bellfounder and the production and tuning of bells*, The Whiting Society of Ringers (2012).

3. Dawson, M.L., 'Notes on the history of Glasbury' in *Archaeologia Cambrensis*, **18**, (1918), p.298.

4. Minchington, W.E., 'The place of Brecknock in the industrialisation of South Wales', *Brycheiniog*, **7**, (1961), pp.1-70.

5. Sedgwick, R.R., 'Howarth, Sir Humphrey (c.1684-1755), of Maesllwch, Rad.' in *The history of Parliament: the House of Commons 1715-1754*, Sedgwick, R.R. (ed), Boydell and Brewer (1970).

6. www.pant.org.uk/Files/history/Tred09_doc, consulted 5/4/2016.

7. Lloyd, J., *Historical Memoranda of Breconshire*, E. Owen (1903), pp.67-8

8. Richards, H.P., *William Edwards architect, builder, minister*, D. Brown & Sons Ltd (1983).

9. Lewis, C.A., 'Glasbury and the Morgan memorial window in Brecon cathedral', *The Ringing World*, (in press).

10. Lewis, C.A., *Glasbury bells and bellringers 1685-2014: a campanological study of a Welsh Marcher parish*, The Whiting Society of Ringers (2015).

11. ibid.

12. Adams, R., 'Fishing in troubles waters: the purchase of the Llangoed Estate', *Brycheiniog*, **35**, (2003), pp.71-2.

13. ibid, p.96.

## Chapter 4

1. http://discovery.nationalarchives.gov.uk/details/rd/ Wood Family, consulted 7/9/2015).

2. Adams, R., 'Fishing in troubles waters: the purchase of the Llangoed Estate', *Brycheiniog*, **35**, (2003), p.85

3. ibid., p.89
4. Escott, M., 'Wood, Thomas (1777-1860), of Gwernyfed Park, Three Cocks, Brec. and Littleton Park, nr Staines, Mdx.' in *The history of Parliament: the House of Commons, 1820-1832,* Fisher, D.R. (ed), Cambridge University Press (2009).
5. Wikipedia, consulted 9/3/2016.
6. Hayton, D.W. 'Jeffreys, Jeffrey (c.1652-1709), of St. Mary Axe, London and the Priory, Brecon' in *The history of Parliament: the House of Commons 1690-1715*, Hayton, D., Cruikshank, E., and Handley, S. (eds), Boydell and Brewer (2002).
7. Forbes, C. no date 'Education in the Glasbury area', www.glasburyhistoricalsociety.co.uk/frameeducation.htm, consulted 20/4/2016.
8. Clinker, C.R., *The Hay Railway*, David and Charles (1960).
9. Escott, op. cit.
10. Vetch, R.H., 'Wood, David Edward', *Dictionary of National Biography 1885-1900*, sourced through Wikisource, 5/3/2016.
11. Ashton Oxenden – Wikipedia.
12. AIM25 collection description.
13. www.coflein.gov.uk/pdf/CPG32, accessed 11/3/16.
14. Wikipedia 'John Tollemache, 1st Baron Tollemache', consulted 10/3/2016.
15. Lewis, C.A., *Glasbury bells and bellringers 1685-2014: a campanological study of a Welsh Marcher parish*, The Whiting Society of Ringers (2015).

**Chapter 7**
1. Bagwell, P. *The railway clearing house*, Allen and Unwin (1968).
2. Lewis, C.A., *Glasbury bells and bellringers 1685-2014: a campanological study of a Welsh Marcher parish*, The Whiting Society of Ringers (2015).

**Chapter 9**
1. Visitation returns St David's diocese (National Library of Wales SD/QA 181).
2. Visitation returns St David's diocese (National Library of Wales SD/QA 186/7).
3. Visitation returns St David's diocese (National Library of Wales SD/QA 198).

**Appendix**
1. Lewis, C.A., 'Premium and travelling stallions in Britain', *Journal of the Royal Agricultural Society of England*, **145**, (1984), pp.57-68.
2. Lewis, C.A., 'Travelling stallions in and adjacent to Brycheiniog', *Brycheiniog*, **23**, (1988-9), pp.75-84.
3. ibid.
4. ibid.
5. ibid.
6. ibid.

# INDEX

*Page numbers in italics refer to illustrations*